From Warming Up
to Cooling Down

From Warming Up to Cooling Down

An introduction to training and management techniques

Susan McBane

J.A. ALLEN · LONDON

© Susan McBane 2007
First published in Great Britain 2007

ISBN 978 0 85131 934 6

J. A. Allen
Clerkenwell House
Clerkenwell Green
London EC1R 0HT

J. A. Allen is an imprint of Robert Hale Limited

A catalogue record for this book is available from the British Library

Edited by Martin Diggle
Design and typesetting by Paul Saunders
Photographs by Horsepix
Line illustrations by Maggie Raynor

Printed by Midas Printing International Limited, China

*To all our equine athletes, who do their very best to work for
and with us and who so often succeed despite us.*

Contents

Acknowledgements

I wish to thank most sincerely Cassandra Campbell and Martin Diggle, my colleagues at J.A. Allen on this book, for their truly professional handling of its editing and publishing procedures, which are always complex and can be unpredictable. Their understanding and attention to detail are very much appreciated.

Sally and David Waters of Horsepix have gone to a great deal of trouble to supply the photographs I wanted. They are always helpful, competent and a pleasure to work with. I am very much aware that 'one picture is worth a thousand words' and I am particularly grateful to Pauline Finch and her two steeds, Fell Pony Waverhead Rose and piebald renegade Nawato Haiatha (Sky). Pauline miraculously persuaded Rose to co-operate for the photos and Vicky Gardner was brave enough to ride Sky to considerable effect. Pat Newhouse and her lovely Connemara mare, Smokey, and Wendy Metcalfe and Bryan Procter's so-handsome Friesian stallion, Eelke Sippes W (Duke), also modelled for us with patience and apparent enjoyment. My thanks also go to everyone else who gave their time and effort to stage photos for Horsepix. Producing photos for books like this is never easy and always tests everyone's patience but it is usually worth it in the end!

Also on the subject of pictures, I have to say how much I envy Maggie Raynor for her talent as an artist and I thank her for being so prompt and co-operative in producing the drawings which have made their own contribution to this book and created an attractive and helpful balance.

Introduction

Some people may think it strange to find a whole book on the subject of warming up a horse and cooling him down again after work. They may ask: 'How can anyone write a full book on something which only takes a few minutes – and is probably not that important, anyway?'

I beg to differ. A horse's entire performance, from going out for a pleasant hack to taking part in a major competition, can be made or marred by the way in which he is, or is not, warmed up before work. When that work is finished, his comfort, well-being and future ability will be governed by how he is cooled down as far as his body temperature is concerned and also by the physical treatment he receives to his body (and, therefore, his mind) subsequently in the form of techniques such as massage and stretching, known as 'warming down'. These processes certainly take more than a few minutes and are more important than many amateur riders realize because they can impact on the horse's performance, attitude, health and soundness. The purpose of this book is to show in easily understood terms how that can happen and how to carry out warming up, working in, cooling down and warming down effectively.

Different experts – such as equine scientists, competitors, veterinary surgeons with an interest in exercise physiology, physical therapists of various kinds, yard managers, trainers and good grooms – often have slightly differing views on how to carry out these procedures, but they all realize their importance and all the methods basically achieve the same things.

A routine to suit you

Towards the end of this book you will find a choice of routines to follow depending on your horse's work and your own time availability. Most of the people for whom the book is written will not be free to spend all day, most days, with their horse or horses. They will probably work full time, or be students, have families to look after or various other commitments which make it necessary for them to juggle their home, work, horse and personal lives. A full, suggested routine is offered for those days when you have the luxury of spending a full day, or at least half a day, with your horse and have time to go into things in detail, either at home or away at an organized event or competition when the horse will be working fairly hard. An intermediate routine is given for days when you have less time or the horse's work is more moderate, and also a simple, short one for times when it is a rush to fit in a ride at all. Even then, it is worth making the effort to spend a few minutes calmly warming up your horse before your ride, and cooling and settling him down again afterwards.

Enjoying learning

Whilst writing this book, I have had in mind amateur owners with leisure horses, who may range from novices to quite experienced riders, whose horses are an important part of their lives. Such owners enjoy looking after, riding and perhaps schooling their horses and, if they compete at all, it will be at local show or Riding Club level, and perhaps up to the lower-to-medium levels of national affiliated disciplines. I hope that the book will also appeal to those making a career in the horse industry and who may be studying for, or have already acquired, preliminary qualifications, or be progressing to higher-level ones.

Learning for its own sake (i.e. not necessarily because you want qualifications) is also well worthwhile because of the knowledge, skills and sense of achievement and fulfilment it brings, so I hope you will learn a lot from the information presented here, particularly if these are topics you have not previously thought about much.

Many owners have regular lessons to help them maintain or improve the standard of their horses' ways of going or performance levels. When your teacher arrives, it is a good plan to have your horse already warmed up and ready (unless your teacher wants to supervise this process). Many people feel that it is a waste of lesson time to spend it in warming up (although much can be learnt and practised during this period), and cooling and warming down are often skimped, if done at all, because the owner thinks that these processes are not necessary after a lesson. Also, the rider has to dismount, pay the teacher, arrange another lesson, put the horse away or out, or transport the horse home (which, to the horse, is a continuation of physical and mental effort). The owner may be rushing to be off home or elsewhere to fit in some errand or other – or just want to collapse in front of the television after another frantic day. This is understandable, but it is not the best way to proceed from the horse's point of view.

The old saying that success begins at home is probably the truest saying in the horse world, and there are plenty of them. Care and management are key, not only to optimal physical performance, but also to the horse's mental capability to cope with human demands. Warming up, working in and cooling and warming down are important management tools which are often unappreciated. The more artificially a horse is kept and the harder he works the more important they are.

Finding a good riding teacher is not always easy but, even when you have one, the tendency is for teacher and client to concentrate on riding and schooling. *Very* few people book lessons in horse care and management and very few teachers suggest them, possibly thinking that no one would want them! The better riding centres run courses in them for working horse owners, as do the many colleges running equine courses, but they are often disappointingly sketchy because of lack of time and the constraints of a packed course schedule.

A schooling or work session (as opposed to exercise), whether well or badly done, can be hard work for a horse both physically and mentally. In my experience as a horse owner and lifelong rider, and as a teacher, most riders – certainly at the level for which this book is written – do not know how to go about it: how to prepare for it, how to plan what they wish to cover in the session (even if they know what the horse needs to be doing), or how to wind it down afterwards. This is not their fault if no one has taught them. Although they may be aware of books, DVDs and videos on the subjects of fitness, work and related management, in the absence of an all-round equestrian education or the services of a teacher who is interested in these things (as well as riding technique) they probably do not understand how important they are and so do not look into them.

Whether the horse is kept at home or at livery, it can be very frustrating for owners who want to do their best by their horses but do not have easy access to correct practical guidance on horse care and management and how to relate this to exercising, schooling and working. The owner working alone with a horse or two at home may feel isolated, whereas livery clients may feel swamped and confused by the conflicting, often assertively given, advice of other horse owners and yard proprietors who may not be so knowledgeable as they seem.

Effects on your horse

Horses are often put to actual work before their bodies are ready. They find this physically uncomfortable and difficult and can become either resentful or switched off, defending themselves against unreasonable demands from their rider. Unfortunately, this is often seen as disobedience. Such horses are also more prone to work-related injuries as the muscles and other tissues are not ready and prepared for the stress of work.

After the session, failure to assist the elimination of toxins (waste products) from the system, treat the muscles to loosen them up again, and even out minor spasms and injuries sustained during taxing, gymnastic physical work, and to settle the horse mentally as well as physically, can result in the build-up of injuries and inefficient physical functioning. The horse can be left unpleasantly tired, uncomfortable and on edge and he will not recover from his workout as quickly as he could if properly managed.

Psychological stress also has to be dealt with. Whereas human athletes understand what they are doing and why, equine ones need help to wind down, rest, relax and recuperate. People working at the levels described above often do not regard their horses as athletes, but they are, and they need to be treated as such if they are to work to the best of their ability, and remain sound and healthy in mind and body.

Further help

The whole point of this book is to help with all this. I intend it to give readers the confidence and independence to be able to make their own accurate decisions on how to proceed at all stages of the schooling/working/management process, with appropriate professional advice and help when needed. At the end of the book is a short list of suggested reading, giving details of other helpful books on this and related subjects. There is also a list of organizations which can help readers source other professional assistance in this often little-understood field of equestrianism. There is no shortage of knowledge available and there are also practitioners and therapists other than instructors, trainers and veterinary surgeons with specialized knowledge of equine exercise physiology.

Inevitably, experts may differ somewhat in their opinions of just how to do something or when to do it, or over the order in which different treatments and techniques should be applied. The information given in this book is logical and based on both study and experience, and is a good basis from which to start. As you learn more, and maybe decide to train in some aspect of caring for the equine athlete, you will form your own opinions. The point is, you can do a lot more than simply feeding, grooming and riding to help your horse's body, mind and spirit so that he can perform well for you.

Techniques covered

The book concentrates on the warming up, working in, cooling down and warming down processes before and after a work session of some kind. The term 'cooling down' is today used to refer to actually cooling down a hot horse, the rest of the aftercare now often being termed 'warming down' by professionals. Most 'ordinary' riders have no idea what that means but I hope they will after reading this book. Years ago, it was often called 'settling' the horse down, which is as good a description as the modern one.

The old practice of wisping (see Chapter 12) was common in any good yard only a couple of generations ago: it is used to treat the muscles after work and after thorough and correct body-brushing (also covered in the same chapter), also to develop specific muscle groups and to give a beneficial body treatment to a horse on box rest. It fell into disuse in most yards because of time constraints. It is now making a comeback and most owners can easily learn wisping (even from a book!) and it is a very worthwhile practice.

The modern therapy of equine sports massage is a different matter and professionals spend a long time studying it and gaining qualifications. As a structured therapy, it has developed fairly recently but, despite this, any sensible owner can learn to give a horse a simple, beneficial massage. The basic massage techniques described here are helpful, useful and quite easy to apply with a little common sense. Stretching is an aspect of this process which many owners are afraid of using but, with common sense and sensitivity, it is quite possible to learn the simpler techniques, and they are important for your horse. Although you cannot have a therapist on your yard every day, it is a good idea to ask a professional if they will give you a lesson in some simple moves if you are unsure.

Although this is not a book specifically on riding or schooling technique, some of that is explained so that readers can understand how a horse should go in order to perform athletic work under weight with the least risk of injury. (This is a crucial point which seems to me to be seriously misunderstood nowadays on a widespread basis, even at high levels.)

For the purposes of this book, I have assumed that your horse is quite well schooled, acceptably responsive and co-operative – if you ask him to walk on he does, if you ask him to move backwards or move over he will, and if you ask him to lead politely in hand, or canter in a controlled way out hacking, only progressing to gallop if you ask him to do so, you can rely on his co-operation. (I much prefer the word 'co-operation' to 'submission' or 'obedience', but that is what it amounts to, with a slightly different nuance to it.)

There is a preliminary section in Part 1 dealing with muscle function, tendons, ligaments and joints and the role of the heart and lungs in nourishing, 'cleansing' and maintaining the body. Basic information is also given on getting a horse fit and on how the horse produces the energy for life and work.

I do hope that this book will set you on the road to discovering more about the vital and absorbing topics of horse care and management. It is not meant for high-powered competitors but for amateur owners who care about their horses' comfort and well-being and would like to know more about helping their equine athlete with a view to using this information as a basis for developing further skills. The books in the reading list and the contact organizations should certainly help with that.

PART **1**

Preparation

CHAPTER 1

The horse's body

No horse should be expected to work beyond the level for which he is physically and mentally fit. Riders need to know not only how to get a horse fit, but also how to gauge his level of fitness so that they do not work him too hard. It helps greatly to have some understanding of how his physique – his body and its relevant structures – works and, consequently, why warming up and cooling down are so important.

The skeleton

The horse's body is founded on his skeleton, which determines his conformation. There are about 210 bones in the skeleton, of very different shapes and sizes, all held together mainly by ligaments. The skeleton protects many of the internal organs and structures of the body and acts as a framework for the attachment of muscles via tendons, about which more in a moment.

Bone is not a dry, dead material. It is made of a fibrous protein material and contains the minerals calcium, phosphorus and some magnesium. As horses mature the protein proportion in bone decreases and the mineral proportion increases. Younger bone, therefore is slightly more flexible and tougher than older bone, which is more rigid and brittle. Like other tissues, bone cells are constantly being formed, worn out and replaced by the body. There are two main types of bone:

1. Compact bone, also called dense bone, an example of which is the hard bone in the outsides of the leg bones.

2. Cancellous or spongy bone, found in short bones and at the ends of long bones, made of leaves and threads of bone. It is also found in the centres of long bones, which are filled with bone marrow.

Bone is significantly affected by work, or lack of it. Fitness is a response by the body to the stresses placed upon it and bone is made fit, or otherwise, by the amount and nature of exercise or work the horse undertakes. As fitness increases, the bone responds to the gradually increasing amounts of stress placed upon it by becoming bigger, denser and heavier. Similarly, this process is reversed when a horse is not in work. This is one reason why it is not the best practice to keep horses confined to their stables other than when they are working, because most of the time their bones are not being stimulated by exercise to remain strong.

The skeleton is enabled to move by means of its joints between the bones. The ends of the bones are covered in a fibrous, gristly tissue called cartilage and the joint is lubricated and nourished by a specialized fluid called synovia, which is secreted by the synovial membrane surrounding the joint. Synovia is present all the time but more is mobilized by exercise. Also around the joint are ligaments that bind the joint together, the whole joint being sealed in a capsule called a bursa or joint sac.

Ligaments

Ligaments mainly connect bones or cartilages and support and strengthen joints: they also support and stabilize internal organs. They are made of fibrous tissue formed into bands, cords or sheets and, like tendons, have a good nerve supply but a poor blood supply. This is why injuries to both ligaments and tendons can be extremely painful and take a long time to heal. A *sprained* ligament (or tendon) is one which has been so violently injured as to stretch or tear the tissues. *Strain*, on the other hand, is force just less than that needed to cause significant injury.

Muscles

It is important to know something about muscles and how they work in order to understand the warming up and cooling/warming down processes, because muscles carry a good deal of the horse's body heat.

Muscle is a heavy tissue, much heavier than fat, which is why horses who lose fat and develop muscle during a fitness programme may actually gain bodyweight rather than losing it. It is the horse's muscles, controlled by messages from nerves, which create movement. Muscles are very powerful but also very sensitive, being well supplied with nerves and blood. Muscle injuries, therefore, like those of ligaments and tendons, can be very painful.

There are three types of muscle tissue:

1. Skeletal muscle, which is the type that moves the skeleton.

2. Smooth muscle, found in the walls of hollow organs such as the uterus, bladder, arteries and digestive tract.

3. Cardiac muscle, which is found only in the walls of the heart.

It is skeletal muscle with which most owners and riders are concerned, especially in respect of joint action and consequential movement (locomotion). Basically, a muscle will be attached to a stable bone at one end (its 'origin') and to a different bone at the other (its 'insertion'), with a joint in between. When the muscle contracts it pulls on the second bone, which is moved as a result, the joint in between the two bones flexing. However, this does not happen in isolation: skeletal muscles work in pairs with opposing actions, and in groups. Put simply, when one muscle works or contracts its opposing partner is stretched, but retains a slight tension so as to control the other's action, which helps to prevent overwork, or the over-extension of joints. When muscles work they become shorter and feel thicker and firmer. Each muscle fibre is stimulated to work or 'twitch' by means of an electrical message travelling down a 'motor' nerve ('motor' because it stimulates movement). Increasing work develops muscles and improves their functioning.

Muscle is the protein tissue we eat when we eat animals and it provides concentrated nutrition, which is why carnivores can gorge on one meal and not need to eat again for days. It contains not only protein but sugar for energy and work in the form of glycogen (a form of glucose) and also oxygen as myoglobin, an oxygen-transporting pigment needed to 'burn up' or oxidize the glycogen to provide fuel for energy.

This process produces heat; the harder the horse works the more energy is produced and the hotter the horse gets. Of course, the processes of warming up and cooling down are also influenced by the weather (the warmer the weather, the warmer the horse will become doing the same work), the horse's body condition (fat is a good insulator, so horses carrying a good deal of fat can find it hard to cool down) and the level of humidity (on a humid, muggy day the air is laden with moisture so the sweat, which carries heat, cannot evaporate away efficiently).

The muscles obtain their nutrients and oxygen from the blood. It collects the nutrients from the intestines and liver and the oxygen from the lungs, all of which are well supplied with blood vessels which narrow down to a network of very fine

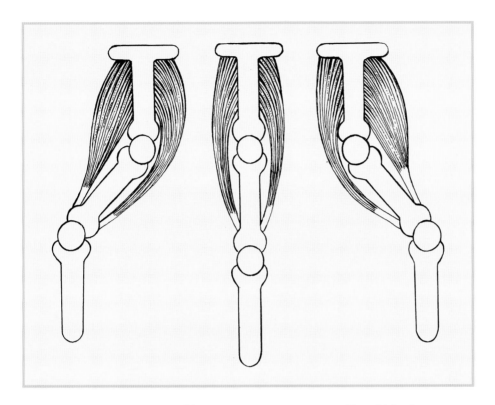

A diagrammatic representation of basic muscle function. From left to right: as the muscle on the left contracts and shortens it pulls on a bone which is able to move because of the joint. The muscle on the right is lengthened but retains a little contraction, acting as a control over its opposing partner. The middle diagram shows the two muscles in equal slight tension, and the right-hand diagram shows the muscle on the right now contracting, with its opposing partner being stretched but acting as a control, moving the 'limb' the other way.

vessels called capillaries. Capillary walls are only one cell thick, so nutrients and oxygen can pass out of the blood into the tissues, and waste products, which are the result of burning up the glycogen (a bit like a car's exhaust fumes), can pass in for the blood to remove them.

Muscles working with oxygen are said to be working aerobically (in the presence of oxygen) and the waste product resulting from the oxidization of glycogen in these circumstances is mainly carbon dioxide.

When horses work fast or powerfully (sprinting, jumping, fast turns, etc.), the muscles use up oxygen faster than the heart and lungs can supply it via the blood, so they use their own stores. They are then said to be working anaerobically (in the absence of oxygen) and a major waste product in this case is lactic acid. This can damage muscle tissue if it is allowed to build up and the horse is not rested at slower speeds (so that he can work aerobically and 'get his second wind') to give the circulation a chance to remove it. This, depending on the levels of lactic acid present, can take some minutes. Working horses too hard for too long can result in exhaustion or collapse resulting from muscle pain and injury, and also from lack of oxygen and glycogen. Dehydration (discussed in Chapter 10) is certainly another factor in this.

When a friend's middle-aged dog suffered from muscle trembling after shooting out of the back door and charging about with his younger companion, her vet diagnosed a probable excess of lactic acid in his muscles, caused by suddenly becoming very active and trying to keep up with the youngster. The vet explained that a sudden spurt of energy and sustained, rapid muscle use before an animal is warmed up can cause a build-up of lactic acid. He also pointed out that this is particularly important to bear in mind for ridden horses who are carrying weight as well as moving their own bodies.

I think we tend to forget that, from the horse's point of view, the weight he is carrying is a top-heavy, often more or less unstable weight which he has to balance on top of himself whilst trying to manoeuvre his own body at the same time – and probably in a way that he would not choose himself. The more the rider moves around or sits out of balance, and therefore interferes with the horse's balance, the more muscle use the horse has to employ to counteract this handicap. This all means that he is using more energy than he would do left to his own devices, and energy use means waste products. His problems may be compounded by discomfort from anywhere or anything, such as his feet and shoes, his girth, his saddle, his bridle, noseband and bit, an unnoticed injury and, of course, clumsy or harsh aids from his rider. An honest horse will try to cope with all this and obey his rider, too – no mean feat and one which can be unreasonably, and unnecessarily, hard physical work.

The vet just mentioned also pointed out that tendons, ligaments and joints can be strained by undue demands before both horse and rider have warmed up. When first mounted, the rider – as well as the horse – is almost bound to be a little stiff. This will make both parties move in a slightly unbalanced fashion, putting weight on to the wrong parts and in the wrong way. One would have to be a super-fit athlete, as well as an impeccable classical rider (and also, probably, quite young) not to be affected by slight stiffness when first mounted. Many of us who are concerned to ride well feel that we are in a better position after a few minutes in the saddle.

After hard work, the muscles' stores of glycogen will be depleted and must be replaced, a process which will take about three days. Working a horse too soon after a previous stint of really strenuous work can over-stress him rather than improving muscle condition and physical fitness. Full recovery of muscles stressed during strenuous work can take about three weeks, and horses should

Apart from using more energy than should be necessary, a horse who is not using his body correctly, for whatever reason, can cause himself muscle and soft tissue strain. Habitually going badly develops inappropriate muscles for the work required, at the expense of others.

obviously not be worked hard during that period. Also, a horse can be sickened of his work if he is made to work hard when still tired. (This is one of the reasons why it is such a fine art bringing a three-day event horse to peak fitness because, after his hardest work on cross-country day, he still has to turn out and jump a respectable show jumping course the next day. Endurance horses undertaking competitions over more than one day are in the same situation.)

The reason for getting a horse fit (see next chapter) is to stress his body carefully and gradually more and more so that it will adapt to the work, become stronger and work better, and delay the point during work at which anaerobic muscle function becomes necessary. We need to prolong the aerobic type of functioning instead, to try to avoid as much as possible glycogen depletion and lactic acid build-up.

Muscle injuries

As with injuries to ligaments and tendons, strains and tears can also happen to muscles, often unknown to the rider. Lameness is often put down to a 'tweaked' tendon or pulled ligament, and 'bad' behaviour when ridden may be attributed to a poorly fitting saddle or a sore back, yet muscles are quite easily injured, the potential being there on a daily basis, and they can be *really* painful. It is not only intentional use of muscles which can cause injuries but such things as violent, instinctive use if a horse is trying to correct himself and maintain his balance after a shy, a slip-up or peck, trying to save himself during the act of falling, or trying to counteract something the rider or driver is doing, etc.

When a muscle is injured, the pain does not always become obvious immediately. During exciting work, the body's natural feel-good hormones and painkillers, including endorphins and encephalins, are circulating in the body and help to disguise the pain and keep the horse hyped up. Although they may not always overcome major muscle over-stretches and torn tissue, they effectively mask lesser ones. Muscular fitness combined with well-conditioned heart and lungs can reduce such injuries.

RECOGNIZING MUSCLE INJURIES

Although horses may show the following signs because of pain in structures other than muscles, those given are common results of muscle pain:

A fall is not the only cause of muscle injuries. Any violent use of muscles, particularly if it occurs in an uncoordinated way, can result in strained and torn tissues.

■ The horse will start to move differently from his normal gait. He may, or may not, be actually lame, but may move awkwardly or reluctantly. It is essential that you become fully familiar with his normal way of going so that you can discern any departure from it.

■ He may flinch when you touch, groom or apply tack to a particular spot. If you rub your fingers or thumb over a suspect area with about the same pressure as

you would use to remove a blob of margarine from a work surface, and he flinches, it's hurting.

- Swollen, warm to hot or tender areas can indicate inflammation caused by injury.

- Refusing jumps or other work he formerly performed with no problem.

- His back sinking down when saddled (often still called 'cold back') and evasive behaviour when you try to mount are sure signs of present, or remembered, pain (not a reaction to cold leather – which is unlikely through a numnah, anyway).

- Standing awkwardly, being reluctant to lie down and/or get up.

Apart from feeling and probing the muscles manually, ways of detecting muscle injuries (particularly those in the deep muscle layers) include using various scanners, or electrical muscle stimulation machines, and watching the horse's reaction for signs of pain or discomfort.

TREATMENTS

The body's reaction to a muscle injury is to protect it by keeping the tissue around it contracted to prevent further movement, causing 'knots' or hard, sore areas. After work, even uninjured muscles often remain in a state of slight tension (contraction) and, if this is not relieved, over time the horse's action can become shorter, stiffer and restricted. Consequently, his athleticism is reduced and the likelihood of further injuries increased. This is because fibrous scar tissue forms to replace the original injured tissue, and may adhere to surrounding tissues (forming 'adhesions'). These tissues will not be so pliable as before as scar tissue is less elastic and the adhesions may tear apart, causing new injuries.

When an injury is detected, a veterinary surgeon will probably advise giving the horse a non-steroidal anti-inflammatory drug (NSAID) such as phenylbutazone ('bute'), or a newer drug, suxibuzone. Physiotherapy is very effective: laser and ultrasound treatments can be helpful, as can electrical stimulation and massage, including careful stretching, depending on the injury.

An in-hand/groundwork and ridden exercise programme planned specifically for your horse in consultation with your vet and therapist is essential for rehabilitation. Inadequately treated injuries can build up and have a knock-on effect in other parts of the body; he may be left with a permanently changed gait plus reduced mobility and performance. Chronic (long-standing) injuries can be extremely difficult to trace and treat, and the horse may develop the habit of moving incorrectly even after treatment, which can lead to other problems.

PREVENTION OF MUSCLE INJURIES

- Get into the habit of looking and feeling all over your horse every day, and of body-brushing him with a traditional short- and *stiff*-bristled body brush thoroughly, carefully and considerately as often as possible, so that you know his body intimately.

- Do some basic groundwork such as simple stroking in a massaging way and leading in hand, at the least, before mounting.

- Warm up before work by walking on a *loose* rein before trotting in the same way. Work in by asking for more gymnastic movements and exercises in a correct posture for the individual horse. Cool down your horse, if he is hot, by walking and sponging with tepid water, and 'warm down' after work or travelling by massaging or firm stroking with the flat of your hands, and performing careful stretches (book a lesson from your therapist) to ease out tension and potential knots.

- Get your horse properly fit. After a spell off work, build up gradually again with a week of fitness work for every week off.

- Don't over-feed energy-rich feeds or protein. It's safer to very slightly under-feed. Go particularly carefully with starchy, sugary feeds such as cereals or young grass.

Walking a horse in hand on a loose rope like this is an ideal way to start loosening him up and is also an integral part of cooling down. Training your horse to walk out calmly and with his head lowered is a big help.

Tendons

Tendons are sheets, cords or bands of tough, fibrous, slightly elastic tissue which normally connect muscle to bone (although sometimes to other structures).

    The slightly elastic property of tendons results from the crimped or 'concertina-like' structure of the tissue, so it is not actually true elasticity. Its effect is to help the tendon recoil when weight is taken off it (a process called 'elastic recoil'). This helps a moving limb, for example, to spring back and gives the horse a free boost of movement as it does not directly involve the use of muscular energy.

left When the flexor muscles of the leg contract, they pull on their tendons and flex the leg via the joints.

right When the extensor muscles of the leg contract, they pull on their tendons and extend the leg.

left Here, the fetlock joint of the left hind leg is taken right down to the ground during weight-bearing, stretching the tendons.

right In this photo, the left hind leg has just left the ground with the help of the elastic recoil of the tendons, giving the horse a forward boost.

17

Tendon injuries

When a tendon injury occurs from over-stress and strain, its tissues (and those of related tissues such as the protective sheath through which the tendon runs), can be torn and the crimped structure disorganized.

Sprained tendons, like ligaments, can take several months to heal and rest has always been the traditional treatment. Various methods of treating these injuries have been tried over the years because rest alone does not restore the tendon to its full, original functioning. This is because the fibrous scar tissue which forms at the injury site does not organize itself into the original crimped structure, so the tendon loses some elasticity. Modern physiotherapy techniques can improve the healing process, however, and in the case of injury to an athletic horse it is worth asking the veterinary surgeon for a referral to a physiotherapist. Most good insurance companies will cover the fees of physiotherapists and complementary therapists – although a limit will usually be set.

The heart and the blood

In relation to the size of his body, the horse has a much more efficient heart, blood supply and respiratory system than do we humans. Together, the blood, the lymph in the lymphatic system and the lungs are responsible for:

- Supplying the body's tissues with nutrients, oxygen and other substances such as medicines and hormones.

- Removing from them waste products such as carbon dioxide, lactic acid, used up body tissues, and toxins or excesses of some substances or nutrients.

- Maintaining the body's fluid balance.

- Fighting disease.

The heart is a hollow pump mainly made of that unique muscle tissue which never tires – cardiac muscle. It is divided vertically by a wall of muscle called the septum and has four chambers – the upper left and right atria and the lower left and right ventricles. The atria and ventricles are divided by valves which prevent backflow of blood during the heart's pumping action, thus keeping it flowing on. The atria receive blood from all around the body in major blood vessels and the ventricles, which have thicker, more muscular walls, pump it onwards again around the body.

The circulatory system consists of the heart and a complex network of blood vessels (arteries, veins and capillaries) extending to most parts of the body. Arteries carry blood away from the heart and veins carry it towards the heart. The arteries and veins become narrower (called arterioles and venules respectively) and eventually extremely fine until they enmesh in a very complex and extensive network of microscopic vessels with walls only one cell thick. These are the capillaries.

Arteries have thick, muscular and elastic walls with an elastic recoil function which keeps squeezing the blood along. As the heart pumps, creating a heartbeat, blood surges through the arteries, expanding their walls. In between each beat the blood flow and thus the pressure on the artery walls lessens and the walls recoil back a little, pushing the blood onward. It is this action which enables us to take a horse's pulse at any point where an artery crosses a bone. The artery often feels like a lively, springy cord beneath your fingers and, once you have found the spot, you can easily count the pulses which are, of course, the same as the heartbeats.

The blood travels on through the capillary network and, by the time it reaches the veins, its force has lessened to a more constant flow. The veins, therefore, have thinner walls and some have valves to stop backflow of blood.

The capillaries are the place where the crucial operation of transferring substances and gases takes place. These can pass in both directions between the thin capillary walls, which are described as 'selectively permeable'. They allow oxygen, glucose, protein, water, vitamins, minerals and other required substances to pass from the blood into the body's cells, and allow carbon dioxide, urea, waste products and other materials for removal from the body's cells into the blood, for eventual excretion outside the body in urine, droppings, sweat and water vapour from the lungs.

The heart and the blood supply increase or decrease their function according to the demands of work, or lack of it. In all mammals, harder work means a faster heart rate to pump blood around the body more quickly so that it can cope with the increased demands for fuel and oxygen and the higher output of waste products. In peak exertion, the horse's heart can increase its beats per minute (bpm) six-fold up to about 240 bpm. Further enhancement of the system is provided by an increase in stroke volume – the volume or amount of blood the heart can pump through in one beat – and by the release from the spleen of red blood cells stored in it into the bloodstream. Red blood cells carry oxygen, so this is another way of providing more oxygen to the system. The body is also stimulated by work to make more red blood cells, and the capillary network itself actually proliferates and becomes more extensive to cope with the extra blood volume and the demands of strenuous work.

The lungs

Horses are 'obligate nasal breathers' – in other words, they can only breathe through their nostrils, not their mouths. For the horse to breathe in, the muscles between the ribs contract, lifting them up and out, and a strong, dome-shaped sheet of muscle called the diaphragm (which separates the thorax or chest from the abdomen or belly), also contracts and flattens. The effect of this is to suck air up the nostrils, through the larynx or voice box in the throat and down the trachea or windpipe, which branches into the left and right bronchi, one going into each lung. In the lungs, the bronchi divide repeatedly into smaller tubes which end in tiny air sacs called alveoli, rather like hollow bunches of grapes surrounded by capillaries.

The main purpose of the respiratory system is 'gaseous exchange' – the exchange of the gases oxygen and carbon dioxide during breathing. Carbon dioxide in the blood coming to the lungs from around the body passes through the thin walls of the capillaries 'wrapped' around the alveoli and into these air sacs, whilst oxygen breathed into them passes through the capillary walls into the blood. Thus the blood collects oxygen from the lungs and disposes of the waste carbon dioxide in the same way as it collects nutrients from the gut and liver.

Since lung tissue is elastic, the lungs are stretched by air intake but breathing out is, in healthy lungs, effortless because of the elastic recoil of the lungs and the relaxation of the muscles just mentioned. However, where allergy and disease are present, the tissue can be permanently damaged and some of the elasticity is lost, so the horse has to make a muscular effort to squeeze the air out, bringing the belly muscles into play to press in an upwards and forwards direction against the diaphragm. In time, these muscles develop naturally and produce the diagonal 'heave line' seen down the lower edge of the ribs in 'broken-winded' horses – a condition that was known as 'chronic obstructive pulmonary disease' (COPD) before this term was encapsulated in the more generalized 'recurrent airway obstruction' (RAO).

The respiratory tract is lined by tiny hair-like structures called cilia, which move in a Mexican Wave-like way to carry out of the lungs mucus, debris such as dust and dead cells, bacteria and viruses up the trachea to the throat. This task is crucial to the horse's general health, work and fitness and in the prevention of res-piratory disease, and is much more easily and efficiently performed when the horse can get his head down. This is why horses should not be tied up short when travelling, particularly on longish journeys (see later this section), and why they should be fed from their natural position – ground level or at least with the poll lower than the withers. Once in the throat, the material brought up by the cilia

If a horse wants to clear his wind it is important to give him a free rein and let him do so.

can be either swallowed into the stomach, where the acid environment created by the digestive juices starts to break it down, or coughed, sneezed or snorted out of the nostrils.

Breathing problems

The horse's lungs are more sensitive than those of most animals and this usually becomes apparent when they are stabled, particularly if in less-than-clean air conditions. Factors which may trigger reduced respiratory function from allergy or disease are:

- Inadequate fresh air in the stable, particularly in many indoor barn-type stables.

- Dust in the air of the stable.

- Ammonia (a toxic gas) from decomposing organic matter such as bedding, urine and droppings.

- Fungal spores on organic matter, which is mainly hay but also straw.

Other factors which can interfere with a horse's breathing and respiratory efficiency are:

■ Lack of exercise and active movement to keep the system healthily taxed. (Being stabled most or all of the time, even if exercised and worked, would not seem, therefore, to be the most appropriate way of managing a movement-orientated animal like a horse.)

■ Tight nosebands.

■ Over-tight girths or driving rollers, especially those with no elasticity in them.

■ Making the horse go in such a way that his windpipe is 'kinked' and narrowed in the throat area – such as with the front line of his face being behind a vertical line to the ground when viewed from the side. (Horses who do not have an 'open' throat conformation, able to take the width of a man's fist between the jawbones, are at a particular disadvantage if forced into such positions.)

■ Working the horse in dusty or polluted areas, indoors or out, where he is breathing in irritants and impurities.

If he is to maintain good health, any horse needs well-functioning lungs for a sufficient intake of oxygen and disposal in his breath of carbon dioxide, water vapour and excess of heat, whether or not he is working. This becomes even more important if he is required to work at all athletically. The factors listed above are irritants to the delicate tissue lining the respiratory tract (and sometimes also to the eyes, which are also extremely sensitive, of course). This irritation can cause inflammation, even at a low level, which damages the tissue and so provides an inlet for bacteria, viruses and allergens (substances capable of inducing hypersensitivity or allergy).

The signs that a horse's respiratory system is compromised in some way are:

■ Coughing more than very occasionally.

■ Sneezing/blowing a good deal down the nostrils.

■ Any thick discharge from one or both nostrils.

■ Difficulty in breathing.

■ A higher than normal at-rest respiration rate.

Horses kept in poor air conditions and those with respiratory allergies are inevitably deprived of oxygen and their entire health is, therefore, affected. They operate below par (even slightly), have less strength and energy, are more susceptible to disease and are generally unthrifty.

The lymphatic system

The blood is aided by the lymphatic system in fighting disease in the body. Lymph is a clear, usually slightly yellow and often opalescent fluid derived from blood, which contains lymphocytes, a type of disease-fighting white blood cell. It is found in the channels of the lymphatic system, which is linked to the blood circulatory system by capillaries which mesh with the blood capillaries. Through these, lymph is collected from body tissues and returned to the blood. However, lymph is not pumped around the body by the heart, and the lymphatic channels are blind-ended. Instead, lymph is moved around by means of the channels being squeezed and released by muscles and other structures during movement and exercise. Lack of sufficient exercise and space to move around can cause it to accumulate in the tissues, very often the legs, which then become 'filled'. Bandaging the legs is not the answer to this condition: the horse needs to be able to move around more.

The lymphatic system is essential in helping to regulate the body's fluid balance by redistributing fluids around the body and for this the horse obviously needs to move and exercise. Lymph also services those tissues which have no blood supply (cartilage, the cornea of the eye and horn), nourishing and 'cleansing' them.

This horse has two significant handicaps at the moment: his throatlatch is tight and the head and neck carriage imposed on him are both restricting his breathing – which is completely the opposite of what is needed by a working horse. He also cannot get his weight on to his hindquaters in this photo.

SUMMARY – **THE HORSE'S BODY**

- The skeleton is made up of about 210 bones of different shapes and sizes. They contain calcium, phosphorus and some magnesium. Bone is affected by the pressures of work: it becomes stronger in response to reasonable stress but weaker when the horse is not exercised.

- Joints are where bones meet. The ends of the bones are protected by gristly cartilage and lubricated by joint oil or synovia. The whole joint is surrounded by a strong membrane forming a 'seal' called the bursa or joint sac.

- Ligaments and tendons are made of strong, fibrous tissue which has good nerve supply but poor blood supply. In general, ligaments help to 'strap' the skeleton together and connect bones and cartilages, whereas tendons join muscle tissue to bone.

- Muscles are the 'meaty', protein flesh of the horse's body. They are very well supplied with blood and nerves, and muscle injuries can be extremely painful. Muscles cause bones, and therefore, the horse, to move. They are stimulated to work by means of electrical messages travelling down motor nerves. Generally, muscles are attached at each end to a different bone. They work by contracting (shortening and 'tightening') so when they contract they pull on the bones and bend or flex the joint in between.

- Muscles contain sugar in the form of glycogen which is a fuel for energy production, and oxygen as myoglobin. The oxygen enables the glycogen to be 'burnt up' or oxidized to provide energy for all body processes. The production and use of energy causes heat to develop and waste products such as carbon dioxide and lactic acid form. Oxygen and nutrients are carried to the muscles by the blood, which also removes toxic waste products.

- The horse uses his muscles not only to move but to keep his balance. The rider is a top-heavy weight on the horse, and to balance this weight the horse has to use his muscles: therefore, the stiller the rider, the less muscle usage the horse has to employ and the better he will be able to balance.

summary continues ▶

- It takes about three days for glycogen stores to be built up again after strenuous work, and about three weeks for a horse to recover fully. Horses should not be worked hard during this period.

- If a horse is showing any kind of 'misbehaviour', always consider the possibility of pain or discomfort, not least as a result of muscle injury.

- Tendon and ligament injuries can put an end to a horse's career. Rest alone is rarely enough to produce an effectively healed structure but modern veterinary and physiotherapy treatments may do so.

- The blood circulates in blood vessels – arteries are strong vessels which carry blood outwards from the heart, taking oxygen and nutrients to the body tissues; veins are not so strong and return blood carrying waste products via other body organs such as the liver, kidneys and lungs. The arteries and veins enmesh in a very fine network of vessels called capillaries which have walls only one cell thick. This is so that substances can pass to and from the blood and the body tissues.

- Horses can only breathe through their nostrils, not their mouths.

- The respiratory system is very sensitive and easily irritated by 'germs', dust and spores, causing respiratory disease and allergies.

- Anything that restricts a horse's breathing – such as tight nosebands, over-tight girths or a restricted throat area – interferes with his supply of oxygen. This restricts the amount of energy his muscles can produce, resulting in poor performance and distress for the horse.

- The blood is supported by another fluid – lymph – which is essential to help the body fight disease. It is linked to the blood circulatory system but is carried in a separate network of channels. It is stimulated to move along by pressure from surrounding body tissues rather than having its own heart to pump it around. This is another reason why horses need to be on the move most of the time.

CHAPTER 2

A general fitness programme

For any athletic activity, the horse needs to be fit to whatever level is required in order to carry it out effectively and safely. The safety aspect encompasses both having the strength to perform the work and also the development of the heart, the muscles and, in fact, the whole body to withstand the types of stress involved without incurring injury, so far as possible. There will always be occasions, however, when even a slight missed step, a slip, a peck or some unexpected extreme movement will cause violent muscle action which stresses and strains the soft tissues – and possibly injures them by stretching and tearing them. In athletic activities this is almost unavoidable but a conditioned, fit horse is less likely to sustain injuries and will recover from them more easily.

There are different kinds of fitness depending on the horse involved, his constitution and the job he is required to do. This is one area where knowing and understanding your horse intimately is essential. Being fit not only enables a horse to do his job but also improves the functioning of the entire body (and also the brain). There are several excellent books on this subject but here I want to give a general, basic fitness programme to help those who are unsure about the process, or who have never made a horse fit before and have no on-the-spot guidance as to how to go about it.

There is no mystery to getting a horse fit. The main requirements are knowledge of how to build up the exercise and feeding and the self-discipline and control to actually perform the routine religiously in accordance with the programme you have worked out for your horse. If you don't do it, or skimp it, the horse will simply not get fit. Getting a horse fit, or 'fittening', as some call it, is something you will learn from trial and error through actually doing the job yourself. You will gain a good deal of knowledge, too, about the warming up and cooling down aspects during the process, and can start to use the various techniques described throughout this book for supporting your equine athlete and enhancing his welfare, health and well-being, such as massage, stretches, loosening/suppling exercises (both in hand and under saddle), strength training exercises, therapeutic grooming, hand-rubbing and wisping. These will be mentioned just briefly here, but a more detailed description of how and when to do them will be given later, in the relevant sections.

Before you start

There is no point in starting a fitness programme or doing any athletic work with a horse if he is not basically healthy to begin with. To do so could constitute mistreatment – possibly even cruelty. It is always a good idea for your horse to have a veterinary check-up every year, even though you think he is in good health. This can involve checking the eyes, teeth, wind and heart, general body condition and signs of good health or otherwise, feet, gait, mobility, parasite burden, and taking a blood profile to give the vet an idea of the horse's general health status. Let's hope there won't be any problems or simmering disorders, but if there are at least you will know about them and they can be investigated more fully. Expensive? Not in relation to what your horse does for you – and necessary in order to be fair to your horse.

This check-up can be performed at the time your vet gives your horse his vaccination boosters. Maybe a month or more before you plan to start your fitness programme would be a good idea: although modern vaccinations do not usually make a horse off-colour for a while, it is as well to err on the safe side and give time for any 'blues' to dissipate. It will also give time for anything discovered in the blood profile to be tackled.

Your hacking grounds

Many people these days do not hack as they feel it is too dangerous. Everything to do with associating with horses is potentially dangerous and, like most aspects of equestrianism, if horse and rider are educated properly and you choose your routes carefully hacking is no more dangerous than any other equestrian activity. It is very difficult to get a horse properly fit if you cannot find roads and/or tracks on which to work. You may have to box to suitable areas a few days a week and work on, perhaps, a horse walker for twenty minutes a day, work around your or your livery yard's land (if possible), do some work in the manège and generally use your imagination as to how you are going to get athletic work into your horse – but it must be done somehow. Manège work alone, in my view, is not good for the horse, not least because it narrows his perceptions of the world and can sicken him psychologically.

A basic programme

What follows is an outline for a traditional, basic, six-week fitness programme, which should result in a healthy horse, starting in soft condition (which means more or less completely unfit, athletically speaking) and attaining what could be called 'half fitness' in that time. This should make him fit for:

- Hacking for a couple of hours, mostly walking, some trotting and a little cantering, plus popping over some small obstacles.
- A half-hour lesson or schooling session.
- Showing classes with little or no jumping.
- Short pleasure or trail rides, and so on.

Thoroughbred horses, Arabs and their crosses always seem easier to get fit than the more cold-blooded types. Also, horses who have been made fit previously and are in the middle part of their lives are easier to get fit than others. Young horses and those who have never gone through a fitness programme take a little longer, as do older horses whose bodies are not as efficient as previously.

The way your horse is kept will also determine his condition at the start of your fitness programme. It stands to reason that a horse whose daily life involves access to plenty of space to move around in, especially to play and socialize with other horses for most of the day, will already be healthily fit. Those who are confined to their stables for most of the day can do nothing towards getting to or keeping themselves at any level of fitness. Horses evolved to live on the move most of the time, walking around, trotting and cantering in play, with the occasional gallop away from danger. This lifestyle makes them fit, as fit as many low- to mid-level performance horses who live a more artificial life. You will, therefore, make your life a lot easier, and your horse's a lot pleasanter, if you ensure that he can take hours of healthy exercise at liberty. I realize that this is not always possible, but it is well worth trying to find ways of making it so.

As a good horsemaster – an older term meaning a skilled, competent and *sensitive* person who has the consideration and 'feel' for how the horse himself is feeling – you must be aware of how your horse is taking to the work. If it is too easy for him, he will not get fit. The body responds to gradually increasing demands, remember. If it is too hard, you will sicken him mentally and possibly injure him physically.

If there is a particular occasion for which you want to get your horse fit, start by working backwards in your diary six weeks and add one week, or two if you like, for unexpected interruptions in the programme such as illness in you or your horse, lameness, lack of time, lost shoes, very bad weather or ground conditions and so on.

Plan your programme in your diary but be aware that it must be flexible to take account of the circumstances mentioned. It is very satisfying to be able to tick off each week as work completed satisfactorily *provided that it has been*. The horse's well-being is far more important than keeping to a programme just because you have planned it. If there are any matters about which you are not happy, consult your vet or teacher.

■ *Start with two to four weeks of walking.* The fitter you want your horse, the longer should be this walking-only phase. If your horse is going to do nothing more taxing than the activities listed earlier, two weeks walking would be enough but, if you wish to go on from there to harder work, three, four or even six weeks are advisable. The first week should start with half an hour's walking

The walking phase of a fitness programme is the important foundation on which the rest of it is developed. The fitter you need your horse to be, the longer it should last.

29

on five days of the week with a couple of days off (but not consecutively). By the end of this week, the horse should be able to walk out smartly – but be careful not to nag him constantly – for forty-five minutes. Gradually increase the time walking out to, say, an hour by the end of two or three weeks and an hour and a half at the end of a month, if you have decided on four weeks walking.

Duke, a Friesian stallion, and Wendy in a good, swinging walk, the horse up to his bridle but not constrained, encouraging him to use himself more and step under freely with his hind legs.

Here, Duke is trotting well up to his bridle, raising his belly and back and using his muscles well.

■ *Introduce trotting next*, initially, in addition to the walking, two spells per session of up to five minutes each, increasing to two or three spells of ten minutes by the end of the fourth or fifth week. *Be careful not to trot on hard surfaces such as roads at anything faster than a steady working trot.* Many people do not trot on hard roads at all for fear of jarring the horse's feet and legs, but others believe that the horse needs to feel the impact in order to toughen up the legs. I belong to the latter school of thought and have made horses fit by including roadwork and trotting on roads and tracks for many years with no short- or long-term problems.

■ *Cantering can be introduced now*, or a little earlier if the horse is responding well. Start with gentle canters with the horse going well within himself at his own speed (remember, you're cantering, not galloping) so that by the end of the sixth week he can canter easily for, say, ten to fifteen minutes twice a session without becoming at all distressed – that means blowing (breathing hard) or sweating much. *Easy jumping* can be introduced around this time.

left Hill work is an important part of any fitness programme. The horse has to work his whole body harder, including heart and lungs, and once he has achieved a moderate level of fitness it can really bring him on.

above Canter work is introduced gently in about week four or five of the programme, depending on the horse's reaction to it. Horses gain most benefit from canters when they are able to use their head and neck (their 'balancing pole') freely, which also enables them to breathe more easily. The author would like to see more freedom in this horse's head and neck.

After a programme like this, your horse should be easily capable of doing the kind of work listed earlier. You can continue in a similar vein, making the canters faster, doing a bit more trotting and introducing uphill work – which always brings horses on in fitness as it makes the work more taxing and develops musculature, balance, agility and attitude. A horse who attacks his hills is a godsend when you are looking for an equine athlete.

Start with gentle slopes and walk and trot up them, only walking down. Keep a gentle contact on the bit going up as the horse *must* be able to use his head and neck fairly freely to negotiate the gradient, but you don't want him pecking (stumbling) or going too fast. Uphill work really develops muscles and activates your horse's 'engine', his hindquarters.

Downhill work is needed, too, but going fast downhill is potentially danger-ous. At first, walk, encouraging the horse to bring his hindquarters under him and getting his weight back. Again, go easy on the contact – gentle but evident – to remind him not to go fast downhill. (In some sports, faster downhill gaits are needed, but your horse must be built up to these and this needs skilful riding.) The hindquarters need to be free of your weight but if you lean too far forward you will upset the horse's balance and may end up tipping over his head if he slows suddenly on a downhill slope. For now, walk straight down in an active but controlled way.

Always walk the first mile out and (possibly dismounting and leading) the last mile home, to warm up the horse and cool him down. After a longish ride,

Cantering uphill is a real test of strength, balance and fitness. This horse is striding out well uphill in a fairly fast canter, with freedom of his head and neck, and is in good balance.

walking home loosens you up, too. Loosen the girth one hole, two if you dismount; this is because, just as you will tighten your girth a hole after you mount because your weight pushes the saddle down and 'loosens' the girth, when you get off and remove your weight the girth will feel tighter and your horse will be much more comfortable if you loosen it off.

Gauging fitness – temperature, pulse and respiration

Always wear a watch with a clear face and a second hand when doing your fitness work, and make sure your rides are the right length for your horse's stage of fitness. Apart from normal 'feel' and sensitivity, you can gauge fitness by checking the horse's heartbeat or pulse (the same thing). If you are serious about athletic riding, you may want to buy a heart-rate monitor. For your six-week programme, however, it should be sufficient for you to use the pulse as a fitness gauge – although the respiration can tell you a lot, too.

A horse's normal at-rest pulse/heart rate is between about 34 to 42 beats per minute (bpm). You can take the pulse by feeling at any point where an artery crosses over a bone, such as just under the jaw or, from the saddle (with a little practise) inside the elbow. Feel for the pulsing action with your fingertips and, following the second hand on your watch, count the beats for half a minute and multiply by two to find the bpm rate.

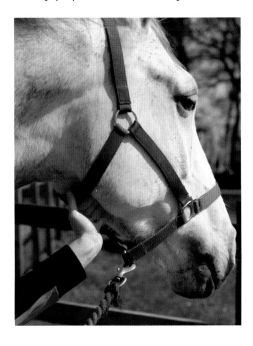
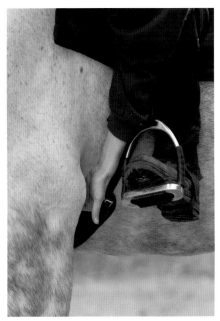

left To take your horse's pulse, feel around with your fingertips until you find the spot where the artery runs over his jawbone.

right You can check the pulse from the saddle, just behind the elbow.

After initially warming up a horse with walking and trotting work, his pulse will be at around 60 to 80 bpm depending on his individual response to exercise. Once faster work starts, his pulse needs to be raised to just above 100 bpm for him to experience enough stress to increase fitness, so take the pulse straight after his canter work or look at your heart-rate monitor. With increasing fitness, the heart and lungs are conditioned by getting the pulse up to 160 bpm and if you want to develop anaerobic ability (see previous chapter) it must be raised to 200 bpm.

After work, cool the horse down by initially walking on a truly free rein (control permitting) for a few minutes to let him stretch properly and get his breath back, then take the pulse. Then trot again slowly or jog around to keep the blood flowing freely for five to ten minutes or so to get rid of waste products, then come down to a smart walk on a free rein. Ten minutes after stopping fast work, the pulse should be noticeably slower and, in a horse fit enough for the work just performed, it should be back to warm-up rate within twenty minutes and to at-rest rates within an hour. If not, the horse is not fit enough for the work you have just asked of him and you will need to go back in your programme a week or two to give him more time.

A horse's at-rest respiration rate is about 8 to 16 breaths per minute, in and out counting as one. Usually, the pulse to respiration ratio will be about three or two pulse beats to one breath, expressed as 3:1 or 2:1. The respiration can rise relatively more than the pulse but if it ever gets near the heart rate, towards 1:1, the horse has been seriously overworked and should have immediate veterinary attention. Distressing a horse not only damages his mental attitude to work but can, in some cases, permanently damage internal body systems as well as his physique.

To check the horse's respiration rate, stand just behind him and to one side. Watch the rise and fall of his *opposite flank* – that is, if you are standing a little way behind his left hip, watch his right flank. Count each rise and fall, indicating one in-and-out breath, as one, at the same time keeping an eye on the second hand on your watch for half a minute and doubling the count to get the rate per minute.

Temperature is also a useful guide to fitness, a horse's normal at-rest temperature being 38 °C (100.4 °F). After hard, strenuous work, the temperature can rise to above 39.5 °C (103 °F), indicating that veterinary attention is needed. This can also happen after moderate work in hot conditions. Humid conditions pose a great risk to horses because they can wipe out the horse's natural cooling efforts through sweating. Heat is lost from the body as sweat evaporates into the air. If the air is dry this works well but if it is humid (damp) the sweat cannot evaporate efficiently as the moisture 'has nowhere to go', and so the heat is not lost so well.

Top equine athletes are sometimes worked in such conditions and their

One method of checking your horse's respiration is to hold a mirror or piece of glass carefully in front of a nostril and note how many times it steams up in half a minute.

support teams of grooms, vets and therapists, with cool water – or maybe iced water in more extreme conditions – and sometimes special cooling facilities (remember the spray tunnels at the Atlanta Olympics) can cool them down effectively. For most of us, working horses at all strenuously in humid and even hot, dry conditions is too much of a risk. No prize is worth compromising a horse's welfare.

As with pulse and respiration rates, your horse's temperature should be back at his at-rest rate within an hour after work, otherwise he could have a problem and need to be seen by a vet.

To take the horse's temperature, you will need a sturdy veterinary thermometer which you can get from your veterinary practice. Hold the thermometer at the end opposite to the bulb and, using a snapping motion of the wrist, shake the mercury down well below the horse's normal temperature. Moisten the bulb by spitting on it or dipping it in petroleum jelly. Stand behind and to one side of your horse and, with one hand over the top of his dock for a firm hold, pull the dock towards you, exposing the anus. Slide the bulb and shaft of the thermometer straight in with a side-to-side, twirling motion. You need to be gentle but confident and firm; don't do it too quickly if the horse is not used to it, but don't mess about. Tilt the bulb carefully so that it is touching the inner wall of his rectum rather than being inside a ball of dung, where the temperature will be lower, then keep it still so as not to aggravate your horse. Talk to him, watch the second hand on your watch and leave the thermometer in for half a minute or as long as any instructions for use tell you. Then draw it straight out, wipe it, and read the temperature quickly before it starts to drop.

Riders who look after their own horses have a tremendous advantage over others as, given a caring attitude, sensitivity and personal knowledge of the horse, they can tell when their horse is working well within himself, whether he is finding it all too much, when he is full of life and health, or when he is off-colour, tired or actually sick or injured. This kind of feeling for your horse is very important for any athletic endeavour, even at a moderate level (which may be the maximum your horse is capable of and so, to him, hard work). This represents the art in training whereas the technical knowledge of fitness and exercise physiology represents the science. You need both to be successful as far as managing your horse humanely is concerned.

It is important to get your horse used to having his temperature taken as it is a vital guide to health and fitness. Horses unused to it often object, so proceed calmly, gently and confidently. Do not stand in a position where the horse may squash you against a wall or kick you.

SUMMARY – **FITNESS**

- Horses need to be physically, athletically fit for the work expected of them in order to work without undue risk of over-stressing their bodies, stumbling and falling, or sustaining injuries.

- There is no point starting a fitness programme with a horse who is not basically healthy to begin with.

- Horses who are correctly fed and managed and who are free to move around at liberty most of the time, and are therefore using their bodies, can be made fit quicker and easier than those confined to stables who can only use their bodies when working.

- A fitness programme must be undertaken regularly and progress made gradually, otherwise the horse will not get fit and/or could sustain injury from overwork.

- It takes about six weeks to get a horse half fit from complete unfitness ('softness').

- A horse's normal at-rest pulse/heart rate is about 34 to 42 beats per minute.

- A horse's normal at-rest respiration rate is about 8 to 16 breaths per minute.

- A horse's normal at-rest temperature is about 38 °C (100.4 °F).

CHAPTER 3

Feeding and energy

We read a lot in the equestrian press these days about the importance of feeding horses a diet consisting mainly of fibre with as few cereal concentrates as possible. This is certainly appropriate advice because horses' digestive systems evolved to function on fibre and their bodies use the type of energy produced from fibre very effectively. This does not mean that cereals are 'bad' for horses – far from it – but we have been so used to feeding cereal grains of various types, and feeds made from them such as coarse mixes and nuts or pellets, that we often still feed too many cereal concentrates, finding it hard to change our ways even when expert advice gives us excellent reasons for doing so.

Natural diets and fibre

We know that horses are 'trickle feeders', which means that, when at liberty on pasture, they eat little and often – most of their waking hours, in fact. You've probably heard the figure of about 16 to 20 hours per day quoted, depending on the quality of the forage (grass and other plants) available. Plant stalks and leaves contain cellulose, a type of carbohydrate that is a natural feed for horses including, obviously, feral ones often travelling around 40 km (25 miles) a day in the normal course of their lives, grazing on and off as they go. Since cellulose is found in grass and other plants, in domestic situations it appears in hay and haylage and all short-chopped, branded forage feeds which can include grasses, alfalfa (also called lucerne) and some feeding straws (normally oat straw, but sometimes barley).

Other sources of fibrous food include root crops such as carrots, turnips, swedes, mangolds – and also apples. Roots or succulents like these contain high percentages of water, but their structural component is fibre. One very popular fibrous feed which also contains some sugar is soaked sugar beet pulp, from which you get a good source of safe energy. It mixes particularly well with alfalfa-based short-chopped forage feeds from the viewpoint of nutritional balance and also because its sweetness counteracts the slightly strong or even bitter taste of alfalfa. A nutritionist once described alfalfa to me as 'like strong tea without sugar'. I wonder if she had tried it?

Fibrous foods like these are digested almost entirely in the hind part of the horse's digestive system, the large intestine, which is like a capacious fermentation vat and home to vast populations of micro-organisms which live off the cellulose and slowly digest it for the horse. Fibre is, in nature, taken in most of the time and also 'processed' slowly by the micro-organisms, so the energy it produces is often described as 'slow-release' energy. Since it has to pass all the way to the hind part of the gut before digestion can even begin, the energy from it will not be released for many hours. Because of the continuous nature of its digestion, this energy is becoming available to the horse most of the time, being absorbed into his bloodstream from the gut and delivered to muscles or wherever it is needed, or perhaps stored.

In natural conditions, equines often travel around 40 km (25 miles) a day, eating as they go for most of the time.

39

Cereals

Unlike fibre, cereals are digested mainly in the fore part of the digestive tract, the small intestine, which comes immediately after the stomach. Nutrients from cereals are therefore absorbed into the bloodstream comparatively quickly and, because of the way we usually still feed horses (giving them specific, timed meals of concentrates often mixed with other things, after the pattern of eating which we adopt for ourselves) they get a short-term boost of energy which runs out within a very few hours; a situation that recurs with the next meal.

If, for example, a horse is fed in the early morning and is ridden two or three hours later, he will have lots of energy for his work – which the rider may or may not want – the famous 'Mars Bar' effect! This can be particularly troublesome when you want your horse to warm up calmly before taxing exercise or work, because high jinks before the tissues are suppled up can cause tiny, or not so tiny, injuries because of tight, 'cold' tissues not yet being ready for demanding work.

Because cereals are full of concentrated starch or 'rocket fuel', they are also often blamed for disorders such as laminitis, azoturia ('tying up'), colic, 'naughty' behaviour, lymphangitis, weight gain or obesity, skin irritations and other problems and disorders. In many cases, it is not so much the simple fact that cereals are starchy that causes the problem, but that we often tend to give too much of this type of feed for the amount of energy the horse is being asked to expend. (It should also be remembered that young grass, particularly in spring and during the part of the day when the sun, and the sugars in the grass, are at their highest, can also cause problems.)

Provided that your horse is actually doing some meaningful work, is not overweight and is starting to get noticeably fit, cereals fed little and often (ideally not in spaced, separate meals) can certainly form a helpful part of his diet – even a necessary one when he is pretty fit and working fairly hard. A lot depends on his type, too; hot-blood types can generally take cereals better than others.

Questions relating to feeding

Let's look at the issues just mentioned a little more closely.

What does 'meaningful work' indicate?

At the start of your basic six-week fitness programme, your horse should be able to get all the energy he needs from grass, good hay or haylage and commercially bagged forage feeds, maybe with the addition of a good broad-spectrum vitamin and mineral supplement (one which contains a balanced, wide range of vitamins and minerals). There are various types of forage feeds, and well-made farm haylage is often very nutritious. As the work intensifies in weeks five and onwards, use a forage feed with a fair proportion of alfalfa in it, as it will be higher in energy than mainly grass-based ones. Your horse may now start to be able to benefit safely from small amounts of cereals, so you could gradually introduce a forage feed also containing a few cereals, and take things from there depending on how he is responding to the programme (getting fit easily or finding it hard work). Do ring the nutritionists on the helpline of the company whose feeds you use for expert advice tailored to your individual horse.

What constitutes 'overweight'?

For good general health and 'condition' – which usually means 'weight' to a horse person – you should feed your horse so that you can feel his ribs fairly easily but not actually see them unless he is turning away from you, when you should see an indication of ribs underneath his skin. This applies to all sorts of horses, from chunky to wiry. Run your fingertips fairly firmly along his side behind his shoulder and judge whether or not the ribs are too well covered and hard to detect, or

Lean, fit and healthy: you cannot see this horse's ribs clearly even though he is stretching out in trot, but you would be able to feel them quite easily – ideal, healthy, working condition.

standing out like guitar strings. If your horse has a thick winter coat, get your fingers right in and down to the skin. If you still are not sure, ask your teacher or vet to give an opinion. Feeding is a fascinating but complex subject and it is worth investing in a good book on the subject (see Further Reading at the end of this book) so that you have a sound working knowledge of feeding for health and how it affects your horse's well-being and performance.

How do I know when my horse is starting to get 'noticeably fit'?

Use the guidelines given in the previous chapter in relation to how quickly he recovers from slightly taxing work. If his recovery rates are not improving from week to week on the same level of work; if he seems to labour when asked for something a bit energetic like a canter spin or some easy jumping; if he puffs and pants after this sort of moderate exertion – and especially if he gets into a sweat easily – he is not coping and you need to discuss his situation with a knowledge-able teacher interested in management, or your vet. On the other hand, if he works well within himself, seems to find the effort required easy and is lively and interested in the world – and also, of course, if his recovery rates are improving steadily – he is obviously doing well.

How do I offer cereals other than in separate feeds?

'How else can I feed them?' is a reasonable question. A good way to feed them on a more natural, 'trickle' basis is to sprinkle them on the top of a generous feed of short-chopped forage and simply mix them into the top layer with your fingers so that your horse can't just pick them off the top all at once (which horses and ponies can do easily with their almost-prehensile top lips). You can use larger buckets, mangers (set with their tops no higher than your horse's elbows, so that he is eating at a natural angle for comfortable intake) or plastic tubs (the kind with rope handles are a good size) and put plenty of forage feed in them, which can replace part of his hay ration. Then, he will take in just a few cereals with the mouthfuls of forage and the rest will fall through the feed as he eats. In this way, as he eats up he will get his cereals over a much longer period than he would in a conventional feed and (provided the quantities are suitable) with improved digestion and production of cereal-based energy but without the dangers of overload. Spread his new-style feeds out as well as you can over the whole day and night in this way and I am sure that you and your horse will feel the benefits. You may need to explain your new system to your livery yard, if applicable, but don't be talked out of it.

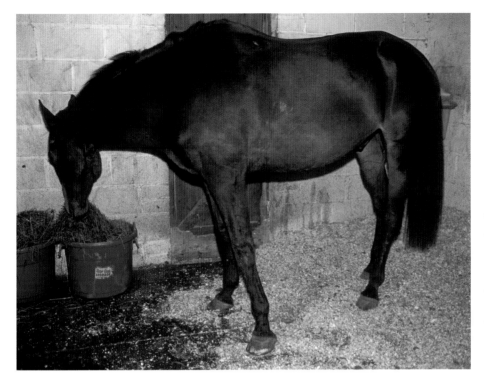

It is more natural for horses to eat and drink from a low level. They normally eat and drink more in this way and are more comfortable doing so. It also calms horses to have their heads down in a natural way and encourages stretching and relaxation of the neck, back and quarters.

What types have the greatest capacity for cereals?

You only have to think of Thoroughbred or Arab racehorses, or other racing breeds with a lot of Thoroughbred in them such as Standardbreds, with their diets of generous amounts of concentrates, to realize that the same amounts would be lethal if fed to many Warmbloods, part-breds, cobs or ponies. The fact that racehorses do work genuinely hard is, of course, another factor: they are in a position to use up and, indeed, often actually require, ample concentrates. Eventers are a similar example. Endurance horses of hot-blood type, usually Arabs, are often trained with few concentrates, but can benefit from them as a quick energy booster during competition provided their digestive systems have been accustomed to them in training.

From this point, I shall assume that your horse is sound, healthy, reasonably well-schooled and that he is about half fit or more, able to cope with work at a moderate level such as various local show classes and Riding Club-type activities, hacking and not-too-strenuous hunting.

SUMMARY – **FEEDING AND ENERGY**

- Horses evolved to thrive on fibrous feed, mainly grasses. Domestic horses, too, do best on a diet which is composed mainly or entirely of fibre of the right energy grade for their work.

- Fibre produces slow-release energy which is sustained over many hours.

- Cereals such as oats, barley and maize (corn), and feeds made from them such as certain cubes/nuts/pellets and coarse mixes/sweet feeds, can be used to top up the energy from fibre in hard-working horses.

- Cereals fed in separate 'meals' such as we eat produce a 'burst' of energy which, however, is soon used up compared with the energy derived from fibre.

- Generally, you should feed your horse so that you can feel his ribs quite easily but cannot actually see them. His back and hips should be well covered with muscle, not fat. This is regarded as good, healthy condition.

- Modern ideas indicate that horses are, in general, better off fed so that they can eat a wide variety of ingredients, as in nature, which are available to them more or less all the time. Mix cereals into large tubs of short-chopped forage feeds so that the horse can access only small amounts over many hours.

CHAPTER 4

Travelling

The journey

If the horse is travelling to his training or performance venue, he should be checked regularly during the journey and, on long trips, unloaded every two or three hours or so to relax and stand or move normally. He may need to drink, move around, get his head down, rest, stale, graze (if possible) and breathe fresh air. This may be difficult to arrange but should be done if at all possible.

It is often not realized what hard work travelling is to a horse. It has been estimated that one hour on the road is equivalent in muscle and energy use to one hour's work. Horses use different muscles to balance themselves when transported which are not conditioned by normal, everyday life and work. Particularly if they are being driven badly and erratically, this muscle use is increased, with the possibility of a build-up of waste products *en route*, putting the horse in no condition to work on arrival. Providing the horse with a small energy-giving feed such as wet sugar beet pulp with or without cooked (flaked, extruded or micronized) cereals as an energy booster is a good plan, with the addition of an electrolyte product to help restore him after the journey. This is particularly important if the horse has had a rough ride for any reason, or a long journey. If he has produced loose droppings, it is advised that he be given a probiotic product as well to correct the disturbance to the population of micro-organisms in his hind gut and so help to avoid the possibility of colic.

Horses should be rugged up fairly lightly for travel to allow for the probability of sweating. Most should have hay or their normal fibrous forage to eat during the journey, ideally from a hay 'well' or holder fitted to the breast bar so that the horse can get his head down, and preferably not from a haynet tied at head height, which will not encourage him to travel with his head down.

It is known from numerous scientific research programmes and from observation that horses must be able to get their heads down below the withers during travelling to allow for the constant clearing of mucus from the lungs and head, otherwise respiratory infections can easily take hold because bacteria and viruses build up in enclosed, warm and humid atmospheres such as those in equine transport vehicles. This is especially important on longish journeys, of course. It is made easier if the horse is tied to a ring level with and back at the withers rather than one at head height.

Travelling in a well-ventilated vehicle helps greatly to reduce this risk, as does frequent clearing out of droppings and any urine-soaked bedding. The bacteria and fungi which can quickly build up in contaminated transport are carried around on the air flow for the horse to breathe in, so he is at much more risk than in a stable.

It has been known for many years that horses generally can balance better in transport if they can travel tail to the engine, either directly facing backwards or in a herring-bone fashion with the hindquarters on the driver's side. This is because the camber of the road will slightly tip the horse towards the side of the road, on to his forehand, which is easier for the transported horse than taking weight on the hindquarters. Horses who brace their hind legs to the sides when travelling are not only standing in an unnaturally uncomfortable position but also stressing ligaments and tendons in maintaining that position. In addition, they are constantly using, in particular, the large muscles in the hindquarters and back to adjust their balance whenever the vehicle swerves, changes lanes, corners (roundabouts being particularly bad as the horse is swung first to one side then the other and then back again) and also during acceleration and braking.

It is not too difficult to find a horsebox that allows horses to travel backwards but, certainly in the UK, nearly all trailers are designed and balanced for forward-facing transportation. Horses do normally travel better, stand more naturally (particularly if facing backwards) and are calmer in a horsebox than a trailer, especially if they are placed in front of the rear axle. This is because the movements and vibrations of the vehicle appear to be greater behind the rear axle, and some experts feel that horses positioned there probably suffer from the equivalent of travel sickness, as do some people who travel in the backs of cars or at the rear of coaches.

The advice of Dr Sharon E. Cregier of Canada, an equine transport specialist, puts in a nutshell how to give your horse the best possible ride, apart from choosing a horse-friendly vehicle and driving on as level roads as possible: 'Drive as though you had no brakes'. Also, drive as much on a straight line and at as constant a speed as you possibly can. In this way, your horse will find it easier to balance, will use less muscular energy and effort to stay upright and will stay calmer.

above left Very many horses appear to travel more comfortably with their tails to the engine.

above Having to brace the legs for balance and security when travelling puts the tissues and joints, particularly the hip joints, under considerable stress.

On arrival

Ideally, you will want to unload your horse as soon as possible on arrival at your journey's end, but a good deal depends on the weather and the under-cover facilities, if any, at the venue. Be careful when unloading your horse and train him to come down the ramp in a slow and controlled way, not rushing or even leaping down. This is because, unless he has been standing in the vehicle for a while whilst you give him a preliminary short massage to ease and tone up his probably stressed muscles, sudden violent movements can certainly strain and perhaps injure soft tissues before you even start.

The horse should have his travelling gear removed and a fresh rug or sheet put on, if worn, and maybe a rain sheet. A useful guideline is that a horse needs one hour's rest for every hour spent travelling: this allows the muscles to recuperate and the circulation to clear out the results of muscle use during the trip, for tendons, ligaments and other soft tissues to rest and for the horse to breathe fresh air.

It is particularly important that, after travelling, he is allowed to get his head down fully and freely during his hour's rest and subsequent preparation so that he can clear out his airways. Therefore, do not leave him tied up in the horsebox or trailer unless he is tied back at the withers and/or can get his head well down over his breast bar in safety. Tying him to the outside of the vehicle, or in a stable, also prevents him from getting his head down, so try to leave him untied somewhere, even if someone has to hold him in hand. (With some vehicles, it is possible to arrange the interior so that it acts as a stable whilst at your venue and the horse can safely be loose inside.)

During your stay, clear out droppings and dirty bedding from the vehicle and leave the doors and ramps open to ventilate it as well as possible.

Obviously, check your horse over carefully for any injuries sustained during travel, for his general demeanour (check his pulse to see how elevated it is – it will probably be at warm-up rate, or more if he's had an uncomfortable ride), and for signs of muscle cramps (stiffness, unusual gait, anxious expression, actual lameness). If you detect a problem you must judge whether or not it is very minor and likely to go with a massage involving slow, firm stroking – particularly the back, hindquarters and thighs – followed by some walking around, or whether you need to call for help. Most good competition venues should either have a vet on hand or phone numbers of those in the area who will come out on request.

SUMMARY – **TRAVELLING**

- Travelling is more tiring to a horse than is generally realized because he is using unaccustomed muscles to keep his balance. On arrival at a venue, a horse should have one hour's rest for every hour spent on the road, before starting work.

- Most horses travel better with their tails to the engine, sometimes in a diagonal position, because they can balance better this way and protect their heads from possibly erratic movements of the vehicle.

- It is important to travel horses so that they can get their heads down and clear the respiratory tract of mucus, gases from a possibly stuffy airspace

summary continues ▶

and also debris such as dust. In a vehicle, bacteria, viruses and fungi also build up because of the enclosed and often warm, humid atmosphere, and perhaps the presence of droppings, and they present a significant risk of respiratory infection.

- Keep the vehicle well mucked out and well ventilated during your trip.

- To give your horse a good, smooth ride, drive as though you had no brakes.

- Encourage your horse to unload slowly rather than rushing down the ramp, and check him carefully for injuries or apparent cramp before starting to warm up for work.

- On arrival, let the horse walk around with his head down for several minutes so that he can clear his wind.

CHAPTER 5

Preparation before work

The processes described in this chapter are appropriate for a horse who has just arrived at a venue after travelling, but are also pertinent to the preparation for work in other circumstances.

Massage

To get the tissues moving, loosened up then toned, the first thing to do before leading the horse around is to give him a light massage by applying comfortably firm, long, smooth stroking, with your palms and fingers moulding to the shape of his body. Concentrate on muscle mass areas but do him all over, going gently (but not so lightly that you tickle him and do no good) in more sensitive areas such as the underside of the neck, bony areas, the sides and belly. Your movements compress and release the skin and superficial muscles and blood vessels, pumping the blood, lymph and energy through his tissues. I am a trained equine shiatsu therapist and believe that massage, as well as actual shiatsu (a powerful but gentle therapy related to acupuncture and acupressure), helps move on the body's life force, ki or energy: I understand that many massage therapists now hold this point of view, too. Stroking the horse in a structured way like this tells the horse that you are 'doing something' to him, not just playing around. Be really in the moment and concentrate on what you are doing, thinking to him about your goodwill and intentions in massaging. Again – *don't rush*. To give a warm-up massage like this will take about ten to fifteen minutes.

This type of massage is called *effleurage*. It can calm a nervous or excited horse or, done a little more briskly, pep up a lazy or 'stuffy' character. You don't have to get too technical or worry about doing it precisely correctly if you regard it as firm stroking and helping the horse to feel good and relieve stiffness from the journey.

Stand not quite at arms' length from him with your feet apart and one slightly in front of the other to give yourself a firm, all-round base of support. For most parts of the horse you can work with your elbows bent but your arms rather stiff and leaning your weight into each stroke as you keep your hands on your horse before continuing. This way you are not actually pushing with your arms and shoulders: it is easier on your back and not so tiring. Do about three strokes in one place.

Create a routine for this. I start on the left side, stroking the horse's lower neck. It is known that firm stroking in the lower neck, withers and shoulder area (as horses do for each other when mutual grooming) can lower the heart rate and calm horses – this is useful to know when mounted, too. Work up to the muscles behind the poll and stroke back down the neck, then massage the chest muscles. Do the forearm muscles by placing your hands around the leg and stroking upwards, then stroke from the pastern upwards and finish with a light stroke

Effleurage is a fairly simple and effective massage technique for encouraging loosening up and improved circulation before and after work.

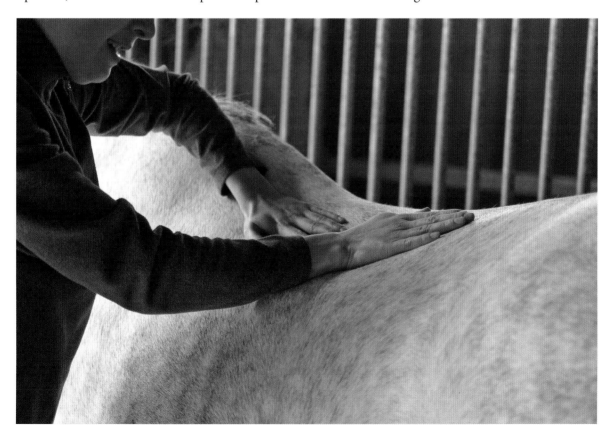

downwards to smooth the hair. Do the muscular area of the back, the sides and under the belly. Do the loin area, hip and flank with more gentle pressure, and be firmer over the hindquarter, the thigh (don't forget the back of the thigh) and from the hind pastern upwards using the same techniques. Go round to the right side and repeat.

By all means talk to your horse, but not all the time as this irritates many horses. We all know how wearying it is to be with someone who never stops talking! It may be less distracting to your horse, who should be concentrating on the pleasurable massage, to be done in his stable or horsebox but it is good, on nice days, to do this outside. Tie him up safely in a quiet area or have a sensible, competent and quiet person hold his lead rope.

If you have time, you can stimulate your horse more, if you feel it necessary, by two more techniques called *hacking* and *clapping*. Do these only on muscular areas of the body – the bottom half (nearest the withers) of the upper neck, the muscles above the elbow behind the shoulder, the saddle area (carefully) which always takes a lot of stress, the tops of the hindquarters and down the backs of the thighs.

Hacking is done with the outside edges of your hands in a careful 'chopping' movement with alternate hands, fairly rapidly for stimulation. You only need to hack lightly to get an effect.

Clapping is done in the same areas by cupping your hands in a roof shape and, again with an alternate action, clapping with a relaxed movement so that your fingertips and the heels of your hands make contact and make a puffing sound as the air is pushed out under the sides of your hands with each clap.

It is worth mentioning here that any movement on a horse that is like a short, sharp impact may be seen by him as equivalent to a warning bite or kick from another horse and therefore, unpleasant or punishing. I always teach clients to stroke their horses, not to pat them, for this reason, and certainly not to slap and thump them like many delighted but thoughtless riders 'rewarding' their horses for doing well. In practice, I find that horses seem to understand that, in body-work, you are using a routine, like grooming and, provided you are not rough with them and speak to them in a calm, confident and low voice, they come to accept that it is beneficial. They certainly learn quickly that they feel better afterwards and relax into what you are doing. However, horses not used to being handled like this may need time to understand what you are doing, so go very lightly and not for too long at first. Watch your horse's reaction. You may feel happier just using different pressures and types of effleurage or stroking, from firm, slow strokes to lighter, brisker ones, depending on whether you are aiming for relaxation or stimulation.

If you are short of time, concentrate on the back, hindquarters and hind legs.

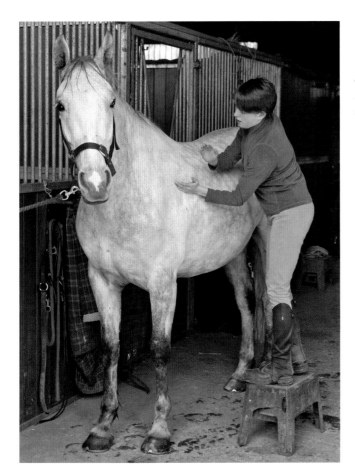

Hacking is a stimulating technique which is applied lightly with the sides of the hands on muscular areas.

Clapping, with slightly cupped hands, is more gently stimulating.

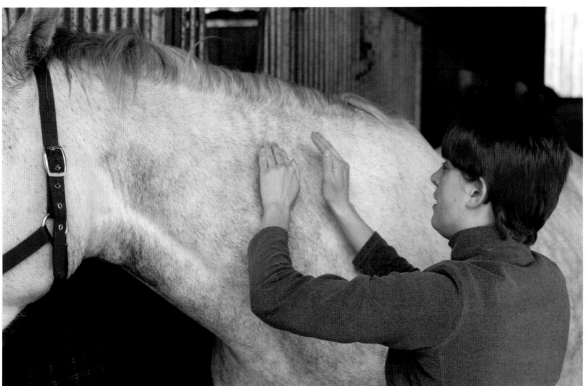

The smell of success

The addition of a little aromatherapy into your massage could also help your horse. Light aromatherapy massage oils are much thinner than baby oil and do not leave the horse looking wet or greasy.

You can easily make a simple general blend yourself. Most health food stores sell aromatherapy oils or you can buy them from a trained aromatherapist. You will need a base oil such as grapeseed or sweet almond oil, to which you can add the drops of concentrated essential oils. The dilution can be only two or three drops of concentrated essential oil to a dessertspoonful of base oil. Do not use essential oils neat unless advised to do so by a qualified aromatherapist. Some, such as lavender and yarrow, can be used undiluted, but check first.

Lavender is good to calm down excited or nervous horses, yarrow for loneliness and insecurity (if the horse is among strangers), rosemary for concentration and peppermint for stimulation if your horse is too laid-back.

Prepare a bottle containing your blend at home (or maybe two, one for before and one for after work, depending on his temperament). Pour a little into your hand and massage it gently into his chest and the underside of the neck where the horse can breathe it in. Try some for yourself, too!

Leading in hand

After his massage, the horse is ready for some movement to limber up. Lead him around in walk for about ten minutes to loosen him up, and start to limber up, rugged up or not, according to the weather. This gets everything moving and swinging – muscles and other soft tissues, joints, blood, lymph and energy. Encourage him to walk around with a long stride and his head low – with the poll about the level of the withers – to stretch and relax his neck, back and hindquarters, which will have been working if he has travelled. This allows fluids to pass easily through the muscles and lets him clear his wind and breathe freely in the fresh air. It should also calm him – although he will certainly want to look around if he is in a strange place to see where he is and what is going on. He may also want to stale (urinate).

If you are reasonably fit, you can also jog or trot him slowly in hand for a few minutes, in the same long and low posture.

Remember to lead him on both reins and to change the sides from which you lead. Also, keep your lead rope loose so that you do not restrict him in any way (but in a manner which will allow you to apply contact if necessary for control). Consider using a long lead lope or half-length lungeing rein for this. This is safer as it gives you more leeway should something startle him, but is not so cumbersome as a full-length lungeing rein.

If in a public place like a competition venue, or where the horse could conceivably get on to a road, I prefer to lead in hand in a nose chain (US: stud chain) – see drawings. If you remember never to haul on it or keep up a constant contact (and certainly never to tie up in it), this gives excellent control without hurting the horse at all. The idea is to give little, short tugs and to train the horse in his stable and yard before venturing out. He will soon realize that it is different and to be respected. You only need to have a horse get away from you once to realize just how little control you really have in an ordinary headcollar. Alternatively, there are various types of 'controller' or 'restrainer' halters you can use, if you prefer and know how to use the different sorts.

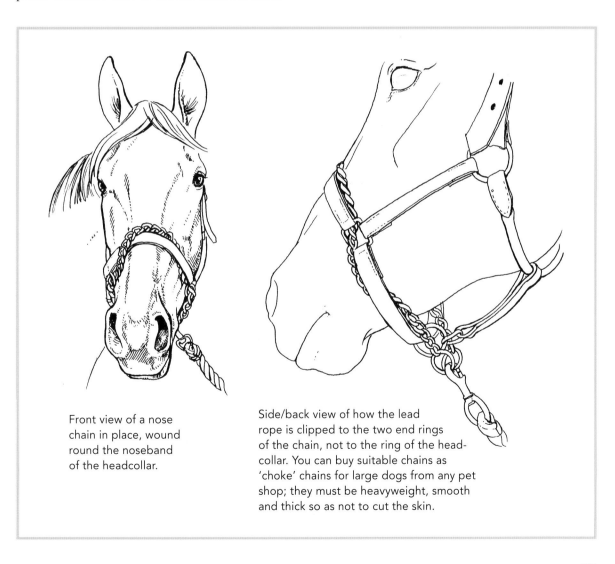

Front view of a nose chain in place, wound round the noseband of the headcollar.

Side/back view of how the lead rope is clipped to the two end rings of the chain, not to the ring of the headcollar. You can buy suitable chains as 'choke' chains for large dogs from any pet shop; they must be heavyweight, smooth and thick so as not to cut the skin.

Many people will lead in a bridle and bit (and it may be that your insurance company stipulates this) but the horse will be more relaxed, and can graze more easily, in a headcollar. I have always found, too, that you have more control, if necessary, with a nose chain than with a bridle and a snaffle bit.

After about ten minutes of leading, if the horse has travelled, offer him a small feed and as mentioned in the previous chapter, maybe electrolytes if it has been a long trip and perhaps probiotics if he has been stressed and has produced loose droppings. All this encourages the blood transport system to remove toxins produced during transit, gets his whole body moving in a more natural way, loosens him up and calms him down, and allows him to refresh himself with a snack and a drink, thereby restoring energy and fluid levels. Attentive treatment goes a long way towards settling him mentally, too, by assuring him of your attention and making him feel physically comfortable.

Excitement is, of course, normal in many horses and you may also want him to have a calming product, perhaps a magnesium-based one or a herbal one. (If the horse is to compete, it may be advisable to check that any herbal calming product given does not contain anything that would contravene competition rules: you cannot just assume that this will not be the case.) Settle your horse by remaining calm, positive and attentive to him.

It is always important to arrive at any performance venue in plenty of time for the horse to have his rest and to warm up. Rushing to prepare him will hype him up and may worry or irritate him, and working soon after arrival simply puts his muscles and the rest of his body under significant stress. If at all possible, let him graze a little: this calms down nearly every horse and, of course, is a source of natural feed for him. Scientific work in humans shows that eating generous amounts of fresh, raw fruit and vegetables enhances the population of micro-organisms in the gut (yes, we have them, too), improving digestive comfort and speeding up the elimination of toxins and other waste – another tick in the box for letting horses eat fresh grass at every suitable opportunity, whether in hand or at liberty. Being with familiar companions or simply being able to see other horses calms down many horses, but you always get the few who are hyped up by strangers and an unfamiliar place.

If it is hot and sunny, or wet or windy, keep him sheltered from the weather – the object always being to keep him as comfortable as possible. Discomfort and anxiety distress horses and then their muscles tense up (in other words, partially contract) in a natural and often unconscious reaction. This is not what you want.

Considering digestion

Imagine that the horse is now ready to be prepared for work after a journey, or having been brought in from the field and stood without food (but not without water) for half an hour to an hour (alternatively, if he is stabled, having had his haynet removed). It is not good to start working a horse at all strenuously when he has recently eaten a sizeable feed, for two main reasons:

1. The stomach lies close to the lungs and these organs can press against each other in movement, interfering with the action of both. This can hamper breathing and digestion, and may result in colic.

2. Blood will be diverted from digestion for the more immediate demands of exercise, again leading to poorer digestion and possible colic, especially if the horse is excited or stressed.

Since the horse is an animal who grazes more or less constantly in nature but must gallop off in an instant when danger threatens, there is some leeway here but, in the wild, strenuous activity is short compared with sustained work and concentration under saddle, and so less problematical. The modern domestic horse's digestive system has not changed significantly from that of his wild ancestors' or present-day feral cousins' and it is more commonly our inappropriate feeding and management practices that contribute to the fairly high incidence of colic in domestic equines. If the horse has been grazing or eating hay, or has had a small feed a short time previously, leading around or riding at walk after about half an hour should be quite safe. Strenuous work is another matter – and some riders can really stress their horses in trot!

So, then, whether you are at home or away either at a competition, a day out or a training session, the procedure continues as follows, with minor variations for individual preferences.

Checking and quartering

Check the horse over quickly again, removing, adjusting or folding back his rug or sheet, if worn, and, following a journey, removing any travelling gear. Pick out his feet and check his shoes, then quarter him to tidy him up. Quartering involves:

- Using a dandy brush or a rubber curry comb to remove any dried stable stains, sweat or mud.

- Tidying the forelock, mane and tail and laying them (flattening them with a damp water brush).

- Damp-sponging the eyes, nostrils and lips and, with a different sponge, the udder or sheath and the dock area (between the buttocks and the underside of the tail). This stage freshens up the horse and cleans sensitive areas.

Quartering also stimulates the skin and superficial blood circulation. You need to use a dandy brush with consideration; you can put on pressure where necessary but don't scrub at the horse as though he is insensitive and you haven't really got time for this. Horses hate being rushed. It hypes them up, worries and irritates them and you need to keep him – and yourself – calm and confident.

Suppling and loosening exercises

These are simple, limbering up movements which help to get the joints free and mobile before asking for more movement. They are aimed at limbering up the horse a little more in the way a human athlete loosens up before starting training or competing.

Because I am a shiatsu therapist, I prefer shiatsu exercises and may recommend slightly different holds and techniques from those of, say, a physiotherapist or sports massage therapist. Shiatsu is a gentle but very effective energy therapy which incorporates some techniques of fingertip pressure to move the energy around and some exercises aimed at the same object and at loosening up the body. A superb book on it is detailed in the Further Reading list. For now, I am going to give you some very basic exercises to start you off and which are appropriate for this stage of a warm-up. They are illustrated in the drawings accompanying this section.

These exercises should be performed after the initial warm-up – the massage/stroking referred to in the previous chapter and, if performed, a little leading in hand. They can actually be done on a 'cold' horse because they make very low-level demands on the horse's tissues, but are all the better for being done on a partly warmed-up body. This is because the tissues are by then warm, lubricated by blood and lymph and therefore pliant. They are easier for both horse and handler if done when the horse is in this state.

This goes for the joints, too, which, when they move, stimulate the production of more synovia, their lubricating joint oil, to protect them and make movement easier. Actual stretching exercises can do harm if performed on 'cold', stiff tissues, possibly causing strain and tears. Massage and/or walking in hand are suitable prequels to suppling exercises.

Important points

■ *As an active rider, you must be reasonably supple and strong, but performing any bodywork exercises on your horse puts different stresses on your own body. If you have any joint problems, possible muscle or soft tissue injuries or significant weaknesses, a back problem or anything similar, you may wish to omit the exercises, and the later stretches, or get someone else knowledgeable and sensible to do them. There are other ways of limbering up your horse, described in due course. Stand as described so that you are in balance and are unlikely to fall if the horse makes a sudden movement. Keep your back flat and strong and bend from your hips as much as possible, rather than from your waist and use your knees.*

■ *In shiatsu, if the horse objects to something three times despite you not being at all forceful with him, work on another area and then return to the original one, when he will probably accept the movement. If he objects again, leave it, try another day, and if he still does not like it seek professional advice as this could be a sign of discomfort.*

■ *With all the exercises, you must be confident, calm, quiet and not at all rushed. Again, be in the moment with him. Remember, your safety is paramount, so go carefully with a horse unused to this work and be content to do very reduced versions of the movements if the horse is concerned. Rest him for a few seconds between each one, fuss him to praise and reassure him, and then resume. Some people would wish to wear a hard hat during these exercises.*

Head, neck and jaw

ROCKING THE NECK AND HEAD

Purpose: to loosen up the joint between the skull and the first cervical bone (the atlas) at the top of the neck, and the whole neck, thereby assisting lateral flexion.

Stand at the side of your horse and put both hands gently but confidently on the crest of his neck, encouraging him to hold it low, ideally horizontal to the ground. Separate your feet to about the width of your shoulders and have one foot slightly behind the other. This gives a good base of support.

Stroke him a couple of times and speak to him to let him know that you are doing something. Leaning your weight forward on to slightly stiffened arms, rock the crest away from you then back towards you, using your whole body in a rhythmic way about five or six times. If you rock to the horse's right, his muzzle will

Rocking the neck and head
This simple rocking movement of the head is easy to do; it loosens up the head and neck joints and tells you whether or not the horse is particularly stiff in this area.

It is amazing how horses like this movement, and how much it relaxes their mouth and jaw, where tension so often shows. Do it with confidence, gently but firmly, and talk reassuringly to your horse as you do it.

swing to his left if he is relaxed and calm, and vice versa. If it doesn't, you know he is not relaxed and calm, or could have some discomfort. Persist gently, talking quietly to him in low tones, and he will soon get the idea.

RELAXING THE MOUTH AND LOWER JAW

For these exercises, the horse's headcollar should be plenty loose enough to allow him to move his jaws and open his mouth.

Purpose: tension is often shown in a 'tight' mouth and jaw, which can affect communication via the reins and bit. This exercise loosens up both and shows that the horse has confidence in you.

Stand at one side of his head with your back to his tail. Put the arm nearer to him under his neck and hold his head gently with your hand across his face. With your other palm, gently and firmly rub his chin and then his upper lip round and round both ways a few times.

Next, slide your thumb up inside his cheek, pulling it slightly away from his teeth (and keeping your thumb well away from them!). Reach up a little and gently grip his cheek with your thumb and forefinger and pull them downwards towards the corner of his mouth and out. Do this a couple of times from each side. I have never known this fail to cause a horse to open his mouth (so moving

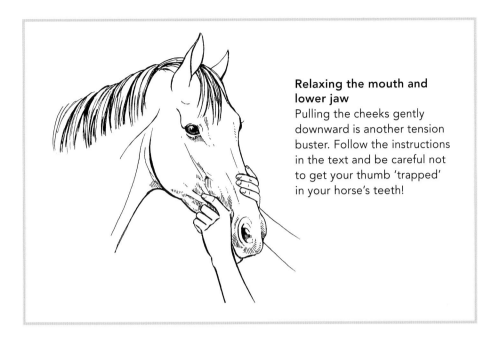

Relaxing the mouth and lower jaw
Pulling the cheeks gently downward is another tension buster. Follow the instructions in the text and be careful not to get your thumb 'trapped' in your horse's teeth!

the important joint between lower jaw and skull just below his ear), move his jaw and tongue around and relax.

The forehand

FORELEG AND SHOULDER JIGGLES

Purpose: to loosen up the muscles and check on their state of tension.

Squat down facing the horse's tail, to the front and slightly to one side of his leg and cup your hands, with overlapped fingers, behind his forearm. Bounce it loosely and lightly towards you about five to ten times, watching for loose movement in the muscles behind the shoulders. Repeat on the other leg.

ROTATING THE FORELEG AND SHOULDER

Purpose: these movements help to supple the joints in the shoulder and leg and help to establish further trust between horse and owner as they are not like the normal movements he is used to, such as lifting his legs when having his feet picked out, or to smooth out the skin under the girth when being tacked up.

Stand next to his shoulder with the front of your body facing his at a slight angle. Place your foot nearer to him back a little towards his head and the other one apart from it at a comfortable distance, so that you have a balanced stance. With softly bent knees, pick up his leg with your nearer hand in the normal way and, as soon as the foot comes up, catch it with your other hand under the front of the pastern and coronet. Place your nearer hand under his knee so that you are comfortably supporting the leg. Keep your body close to his leg and hold the cannon horizontal to the ground. His knee will be forward and this should be quite comfortable for him.

Holding the leg comfortingly, move your body in a circular manner towards his body, round and away and back again, taking his leg with you. Start with a slight circular movement about 15 cm (6 in) in diameter and gradually increase its size to about 30 cm (12 in) over eight or ten circles, then do the same in the other direction. Repeat with the other foreleg. Place each leg down with both hands at the pastern and fetlock (making sure you do not get your fingers trodden on) rather than letting the horse take it from you and drop it.

This exercise not only relaxes the muscles and mobilizes soft tissues in the shoulder and surrounding area, but also starts to open up the point-of-shoulder and elbow joints whilst flexing the knee, moving fluids and energy.

After these rotations, do the foreleg jiggles again and you should see an increase and improvement in the looseness of the shoulder muscles.

Foreleg and shoulder jiggles
Watch the muscles behind the horse's shoulder to see how much they move (which indicates how relaxed the horse is) when you do the foreleg and shoulder jiggles.

Rotating the foreleg and shoulder
Hold your horse's forearm close to your upper body in a comfortable, reassuring hold as you move his leg and shoulder gently in a horizontal, circular movement.

FOOT ROTATIONS AND FLEXIONS

Purpose: to loosen up the foot and lower leg joints and tissues, stimulate circulation and energy flow and the production of synovia.

Pick up the foreleg, squat down and rest it at the fetlock across your thigh near your knee with the cannon horizontal to the ground. Hold the pastern securely and comfortably with one hand and the toe resting in your other palm. Moving your body from your stomach area (your 'centre' in oriental modalities), slowly rotate the foot with the hand holding the toe four or five times in each direction *without* forcing it.

Next, raise the foot up towards the elbow and, with the flat of your hand on the bottom of the foot, gently press it down again to put the joints through their range of motion, again without force. Repeat with the other foreleg.

RAISED FORELEG SWING

Purpose: mobilizes the shoulder, elbow and forearm laterally.

Whilst still in your squatting position from the previous exercise and still resting the leg on your thigh/knee, place one hand on the front of his knee and the other under the wall of his hoof. Using your body again and the hand on his knee (keeping his foot still with the other), gently and slowly swing your body (from your centre) and his knee towards and away from you a few times – but don't actually push the knee – just take it with you. The object is to open the elbow so

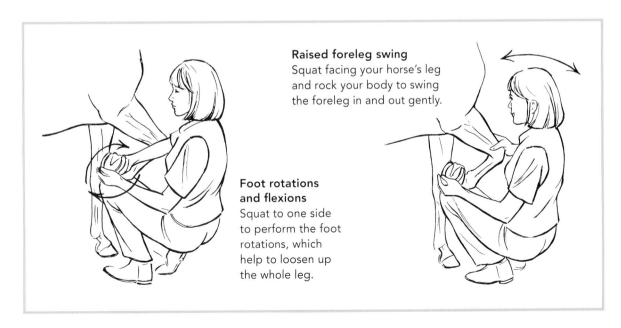

Raised foreleg swing
Squat facing your horse's leg and rock your body to swing the foreleg in and out gently.

Foot rotations and flexions
Squat to one side to perform the foot rotations, which help to loosen up the whole leg.

that the shoulder moves laterally with your body, then back again. Gradually reduce the movement and place the foot on the ground as described above. Repeat the whole sequence, then do it with the other foreleg.

If you do not want to squat for the above exercises, it is possible to do them standing, with softly bent knees, provided you support the leg properly with both hands, as described, and stay close to the horse with your body, both for reassurance for him and for your own balance.

At this point, it is a good idea to lead your horse around for a minute or so in walk so that he can feel and get used to his loosened-up forehand, before carrying on.

Pre-work stretching exercises

As stated above, it is essential that, before full warm-up, 'cold' tissues are not stretched to the end of their range, as injuries such as strains and torn tissues can happen easily and can be made worse by the fact that the horse is likely to resist and pull against you. The stretches described here are to *start* to extend the tissues and joints only as far as is comfortable for the horse. All animals and people love a good stretch after they have been in a sedentary or cramped position and this is both necessary and beneficial *provided it is not overdone.*

Foreleg and shoulder

Purpose: to extend the leg and shoulder gently forwards and backwards to prepare them for more demanding work.

FORWARD STRETCH

Stand just in front of your horse's shoulder with the front of your body facing it at a slight angle. Pick up the leg as described for the previous set of exercises and spread your feet again for good balance, your foot nearer the horse back a little and your other foot forwards. Support the horse's leg under the knee with your outside hand and under the fetlock with your inside hand: this hold feels comfortable and reassuring to him, encouraging co-operation and balance and lessening the stretch down the back of the leg.

Holding the leg comfortably and directly in front of the shoulder, take your body and weight backwards on to your inside leg, knees comfortably bent, bringing the leg with you *only so far as the horse agrees.* Do not actually pull the leg or try to force a stretch. You can hold this position for five to ten seconds, during which time the horse may, or may not, lean backwards and stretch the leg more himself. Be sensitive to what he wants. Put his leg down in the correct way, as described earlier, and stroke him. Repeat with the other leg.

BACKWARD STRETCH

Stand at the horse's shoulder, again facing it but slightly angled towards the tail, with your feet apart, and pick up the foot/leg as before. The horse's instinct is to angle the forearm forwards so, placing your nearer hand on the front of his knee and supporting his fetlock joint underneath with the other hand, let him do so. The first time or two you do backward stretches just gently encourage him to take his forearm back until it is vertical to the ground (no further), by pushing on his knee, keeping the cannon horizontal to the ground. (Some people use the squatting position for this and support the leg on their knee.) The tissues down the front of the forearm and in the shoulder will be very slightly stretched and mobilized, and the upper joints extended. At first, hold for only two or three seconds.

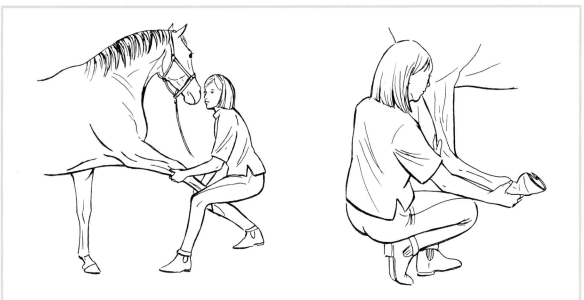

Forward stretch
Stretching the foreleg forward is something done often, if only to smooth out the skin under the girth, but it is frequently overdone. For comfort and reassurance for your horse, follow the instructions in the text.

Backward stretch
Very few horses are used to having their forelegs stretched backwards. Again, follow the text. Most practitioners like to rest the leg on their knee and just keep the forearm vertical and the cannon horizontal at first, in a right angle. As the horse gets more used to it, gently push the knee back a little, but do let the lower leg and hoof drop closer to the ground so that you do not overdo the stretch and cause discomfort and resistance in your horse.

As he gets used to this exercise, push the knee a little further back and *take the foot lower towards the ground* to keep him comfortable and within his normal range of movement. Place the foot on the ground and praise him. Repeat with the other leg.

The hind legs and hindquarters

HIND LEG SWING

Purpose: to relax the area in readiness for the next exercises.

Ask your horse to stand with his hind leg relaxed, hip dropped, by lifting it and putting it down again, resting on the toe. This will take a little working out on the horse's part, but if you are calm and patient he will catch on. This makes the leg and hindquarter on that side loose and relaxed.

Squat down facing his leg and place your hands around his leg just above the hock joint. With a loose, swinging movement, using your body, swing his leg to left and right a few times.

BACK FOOT ROTATION

Purpose: to loosen up the joint and tissues and prepare the horse for the exercise which follows it.

Following on from the previous exercise, stand up taking the usual stance with your feet apart and pick up the foot, supporting it with your nearer hand under the pastern and coronet and holding the toe with your outside hand. With that hand, rotate the foot slowly four or five times in each direction. Then gently lift and press the foot up and back towards the fetlock and, with your palm on the underside of the foot, press it down again to flex and extend the joint.

HIND LEG ROTATIONS

Purpose: to loosen up the joints in the hindquarter and leg, and surrounding tissues.

Stand facing the horse's tail and slightly facing the hind leg, and pick up the leg with your inside arm under the hock, holding the leg under the fetlock joint and hoof, and keeping it directly below his hip. Take up your feet-apart stance and, almost as though you are hugging his leg, move your body – and his foot – in small circles horizontal to the ground. Take his leg backwards a little and rotate again in slightly larger circles then, if the horse is fine with this, back just a little further, still rotating, in circles no more than about 40 cm (16 in) diameter.

If you and he are happy, you can stop rotating, maintain your comfortable, secure hold on his leg and move on to the next exercise.

HIND LEG STRETCHES

Purpose: to extend the leg and hip *gently* forward and backward and prepare them for more demanding work.

BACKWARD HIND LEG STRETCH

Staying in your feet-apart stance from the previous exercise, lean your weight forwards slowly on to your forward foot and just take the horse's leg straight back with you *without* pulling it or angling it. This is a natural progression and many horses will stretch the leg beyond what you are asking. If the horse resists your gentle efforts, just hold passively and talk to him and he will almost certainly give

Hind leg swing
This is the hind leg swing; you rock your body gently towards and away from the leg, bringing it with you as you go. As with the foreleg/shoulder jiggles, watch the thigh muscles to see how much relaxation the horse is showing.

Hind leg stretches
Stretching the hind leg backwards, like other moves, is best done holding the leg close to your upper body for security and comfort.

you the leg. Try to hold it for two or three seconds; he is probably not used to this, remember.

He may immediately try to take the leg back and stamp it down and you may need to let go. However, talk to him and try to come back with more weight on your rear foot, bringing his leg with you, and *put* the foot down rather letting him drop or stamp it down. Praise him if he co-operates in this. Repeat the exercise on the other leg.

As he gets used to this bodywork, you should have no problems in respect of co-operation, but don't force the issue. Go slowly over the days and never let an argument develop; do just what he is comfortable with, praise him for good results and he will progress and learn to work with you.

FORWARD HIND LEG STRETCH

Stand just in front of the horse's hip, slightly facing it, and pick up his leg and foot, supporting the fetlock with one hand underneath it and the other as shown below, slightly up the cannon. Bringing the leg directly forward, move your body-weight on to your back foot and bring the leg forwards with you, straight towards the front hoof. As usual, do not pull or force the stretch. Try to hold it for two or three seconds, building up over the weeks to ten seconds. Speak calmly to the horse, take the leg back to its vertical stance position and put the foot down. Praise him. Repeat the exercise with the other leg.

Now walk him quietly around for a minute to let him feel his own body and action after this work.

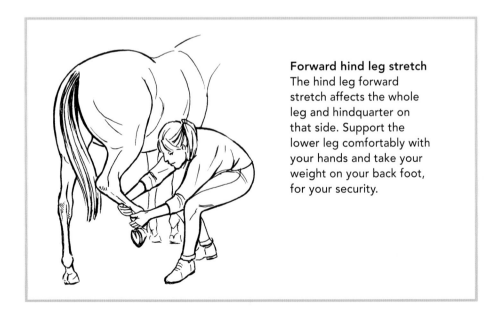

Forward hind leg stretch
The hind leg forward stretch affects the whole leg and hindquarter on that side. Support the lower leg comfortably with your hands and take your weight on your back foot, for your security.

The tail

You can proceed to working on the tail if you have time and provided the horse does not kick. If he does kick or resents having his tail handled, just trying a gently 'pulling stroke' down his dock from the side can get him used to it, and you can then try to progress over time. If he (or, more likely, a mare) cow-kicks, even this may not be possible, but some training will need to be done at some point if only to enable you to groom the tail and clean underneath it, or take the temperature when necessary.

Purpose: many people are surprised that manipulating the tail can serve any purpose. However, the tail is part of the spine and the end of the spinal cord runs down inside the upper tail vertebrae. Working the tail correctly benefits the whole back and most horses (even those who are sensitive about their tails), enjoy it once they get used to it.

SIDEWAYS MOVE

Stand just in front of the horse's hip facing his tail and place your palms on the dock with your fingers underneath it. Bring it towards you gently with just a little tension on it, then, keeping hold of it, walk round to the other side, change your hold accordingly and repeat. Most horses place their weight on the side to which you place the tail, moving with you.

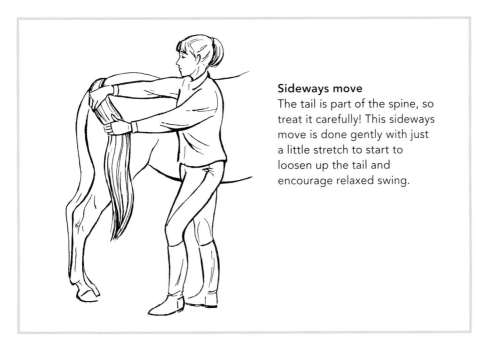

Sideways move
The tail is part of the spine, so treat it carefully! This sideways move is done gently with just a little stretch to start to loosen up the tail and encourage relaxed swing.

ROTATING THE TAIL

Standing behind the horse, and to one side. Place the palm of one hand under the very top of his tail, with your thumb curling round on top one way and your fingers the other. Place your other hand similarly about a hand's width down from your top hand and hold around the dock. Gently and slowly just circle the root of the tail two or three times in each direction.

Move your hands gradually down the dock, holding the tail securely with your top hand and rotating each vertebra gently with the lower hand.

With your top hand still under the tail, but your lower hand now over it, gently arch the tail a little with your top hand and hold it there whilst slightly pulling down on the dock with your other hand, moving down the dock like this for about two-thirds of its length.

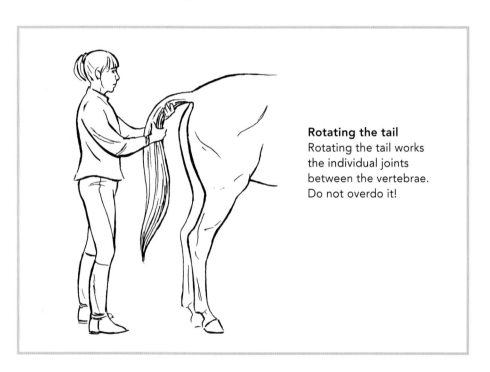

Rotating the tail
Rotating the tail works the individual joints between the vertebrae. Do not overdo it!

STRETCHING THE TAIL

Purpose: to very slightly stretch the tail and the whole spine and surrounding tissues.

Stand immediately behind your horse, holding his dock with both hands from underneath, one hand higher than the other. Stand with one foot behind the other and lean your weight on to your back foot so that your horse feels a pull on

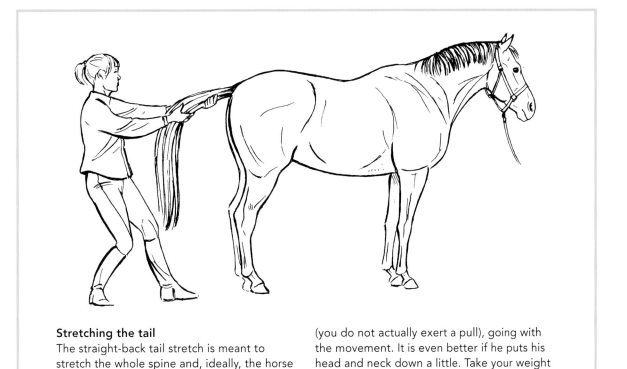

Stretching the tail
The straight-back tail stretch is meant to stretch the whole spine and, ideally, the horse will lean forwards slightly against your weight (you do not actually exert a pull), going with the movement. It is even better if he puts his head and neck down a little. Take your weight on your back foot, then release it slowly.

his tail (even though you are not actually pulling). He will probably lean forwards against this feeling, stretching along his whole spine: this is even better if you have someone in front of him encouraging him to lower his head a little.

Hold this for five to ten seconds, if he is happy with it, and then *slowly* pull yourself towards him, taking your weight on your front foot, and gradually release the tension.

Before you began these suppling exercises, you will have massaged or stroked your horse. As well as starting to treat and loosen up the tissues and get the blood and lymph flowing, it will have stimulated the flow of ki (energy) from a shiatsu viewpoint. To finish a session, it is advised by many shiatsu and acupressure therapists to just stroke the body all over again to 'close him down'. After this, I lift the dock between my two hands, let the hair run through them right to the ends and fall against his hind legs. This acts as a sign to him that the session is over, a sign that he remembers every time afterwards.

This routine, done after massage and initial leading in hand, will prepare him well for more taxing work on the ground, which is the next stage of this suggested programme of preparation.

SUMMARY – **PREPARATION BEFORE WORK**

- After leading around on arrival at a show (or if he has been stabled), give your horse a massage to ease his muscles and get the blood flowing, maybe with appropriate aromatherapy oils. Then lead around again for about ten minutes to loosen him up further.

- Offer your horse a drink, maybe with electrolytes added if he has sweated up whilst travelling, and a small, nourishing and easily-digested feed. If his droppings have been loose during the journey, consider giving him a dose of probiotic to settle his hind gut and ward off future problems. If he is the nervous or excitable type, maybe a nutritional or herbal calming product would help him.

- Check the horse over again, quarter him and then do the suppling/loosening up exercises to start to prepare him for physical effort.

CHAPTER 6

Lungeing, long-reining and work in hand

Having carried out massage and stretching exercises, the objective now is to get the horse more actively loosened up by means of lungeing, long-reining and/or work in hand, to get everything flowing in readiness for mounting. It is quite possible, of course, to skip this part and go straight on to warming up under saddle on a loose rein, but it is more effective to do some careful work on the ground first if you have the time and if the mounted work is going to be at all demanding.

Lungeing

Lungeing is a very popular and common way of warming up horses before work but it is often done wrongly, and so badly that it is actually harmful to the horse's body. Horses learn very quickly and soon form habit patterns, and they may automatically move wrongly if started off that way. They can also get the wrong mental attitude towards it.

Equipment and facilities

The right and beneficial way to lunge a horse for warming up is in a relaxed way so that he can move and use his body naturally, in simple tack such as a strong lungeing cavesson and with no other equipment or training aids.

However, some prefer to lunge from a bridle and use various ways of fastening the rein to the bit. Try different methods to see which suits the horse best.

- You can simply clip it to the inside bit ring – although I think this feels pretty unstable.

- You can clip the rein to the outside bit ring, pass it (flat) over the poll and back down through the inside bit ring.

- You can pass the clip through the inside bit ring, under the horse's chin and fasten it to the outside bit ring.

Note that lungeing from a bridle and bit is not a technique to be used by the heavy-handed or the inexperienced. Get someone used to it and good at it to show you and supervise you until you are competent enough yourself.

It is important that the horse should be allowed free use of his head and neck so that his body can operate as a whole and really move in a limbering-up way. Also, it is essential for him to be comfortable in his tack: unnecessary discomforts such as a tight noseband, bit adjusted too high, headpiece rubbing the ears and so on can distract the horse and put him off his work.

You can either remove the reins (my preference) or fasten them up safely by giving them a couple of twists under the horse's neck and passing the throatlatch through the twist to hold them up.

Using a lungeing whip is optional and many people don't bother with one if their horse lunges well. A schooling whip is a reasonable guide, particularly if you paint it white. Horses can see this clearly and you can point to parts of the horse to help control him – quarters to move him on, shoulders to slow him or keep him out, head to stop him. With a little sensible training and practice, it is not that difficult.

If you are in the habit of leading your horse in hand for warming up, you will know how important it is to have a surface that is not too deep (with the risk of soft tissue strain as the horse struggles to get his feet out of it), holding (with the same result plus the possibility of loosening or pulling off shoes), hard (risk of concussion), dead (with no spring in it and quite hard work) or, of course, slippery. Therefore, choose your lungeing surface carefully and, if you are in a strange place, try it out by walking and running on it yourself first, if necessary. You will also probably want to put protective boots on your horse before you start.

Starting off

Begin in your long, low walk as an extension of leading in hand. Keep the rein looped in your hand (*never wrapped round it or with your wrist through the loop, in case the horse takes off*) and walk with your horse, gradually getting further from him. Forget about keeping only to a circle with you standing rigidly in the

middle. Walk with him on straight lines, ovals and *big* circles, almost to the end of the line, only retaining enough to give you some slack in an emergency such as him getting startled. Build up to this and do it on both reins for five or ten minutes. He will soon get the message.

Small circles are a difficult exercise and only fit, agile and quite highly schooled horses can perform them correctly. Others invariably bank (lean in) on the circle with the head out in a desperate effort to balance, stressing the legs (particularly the inside ones), and doing themselves quite a lot of harm both mentally and physically. These ill-effects are obviously increased the faster the horse goes.

When you start the horse trotting (he should obey your voice commands) keep it to little more than a jog at first, still with the head low, and progress to a steady, careful working trot. This is no time to let him display high jinks and get the itch out of his heels. Strong or even violent movements during a warm-up are asking for stretched, torn and stressed tissues and can certainly do more harm than good. This is partly where so many people go wrong. The horse thinks 'yippee – playtime' and may then do so forever more. Once a horse is warmed up, then he can play around, if you like, but make sure that he is sufficiently obedient to your voice aids to stop it when you say so. Establish this habit and you should have no problems.

This is a beautiful example of a horse being lunged to loosen him up and encourage him to move freely, with his head down, back lifting, quarters under and hind legs working actively in good form, with no equipment other than a cavesson. Note the large circle.

Another important point is *not* to ask or let the horse whiz round in trot like a maniac. So many people think that this is warming up and settling him down before work. It is not. It gives him the mind-set of powering off in trot before his body is ready and he will then do it every time. It can be quite difficult to retrain such a horse to trot slowly or moderately in a beneficial posture and to listen to your requests, so don't let it start. Fast work like this, whether in trot or canter, and especially on small circles, can cause physical stress and strain.

If you have a horse who already does this, you may have to start him again from scratch, teaching absolute obedience to the voice, maybe with the help of your teacher. His instant response to a command to stop or slow down must be well ingrained as a habit. Practise this leading in hand at walk and trot, then progress to lungeing in walk, staying fairly close to him, and checking his responses. Next, ask for a very slow trot. This is when most horses with this habit charge off. If this happens, immediately give the slow down or even stop command, and keep repeating this until he gets the habit, instead, of trotting in a calm way. You need some means of letting him know that this is good behaviour and applying it *the instant* he gets it right. Some people like clicker training, some use a pleased-sounding 'good boy', but whatever you use, make sure it is instant or within a couple of seconds at most, or he will not get the message.

Exercises

Exercises you can perform on the lunge are:

- Large circles, not smaller than 20 m for this type of work.

- Straight lines and ovals (walking with the horse).

- Correct, fairly frequent transitions up and down for all gaits and including halt, not rushed with the head up but aiming for good use of the hindquarters; the horse's back up and the head and neck slightly stretched forward and down.

- Try reining-back on the lunge for just a couple of steps and then moving the horse immediately forward again; if he doesn't comply with the request to step back, just tap him on the chest (don't push him back by the head, which won't do him any good at all) and say 'back' or whatever he understands.

- If your horse is obedient on the lunge, work on a slight slope up and down, for balance, co-ordination and, like transitions, to encourage engagement and thrust of the hindquarters, a raised belly and back, and good balance.

You can also ask the horse for a couple of loose, easy canters on the lunge along the above lines, keeping him steady, and by then – say after about fifteen minutes – he will be warmed up. Check his pulse; it should be about 60–80 bpm. Remember to finish the lungeing spell with walking out freely, head down, for a few minutes.

TTEAM lungeing

A useful method of lungeing, which I like, is TTEAM lungeing (Tellington Touch Equine Awareness Method), which is simple to learn (see Useful Contacts at the end of this book) and a sort of part-way between leading in hand and conventional lungeing (my definition). You use a long lead or half-length lungeing rein and the Tellington 'wand' (a white schooling whip). The accompanying drawing shows the technique but, basically, you hold the lead and the wand in the same hand, the one nearer your horse, and walk or run more with the horse. You can use the wand to direct your horse with a simple movement of your wrist to point it where you need it.

If you use a lungeing cavesson, use the front central ring for the rein so that you do not have to keep changing the fitting when you change direction. Alternatively, you can buy proper Tellington leads to use with an ordinary headcollar, which are fitted as shown on page 78: the long lead has a length of chain or soft, covered rope on one end, with a clip. If you are working from the left side, you pass the clip through the left side dee and over the horse's nose, wrapping the rope around it once. Take the clip through the right side dee and up the right side of the face, clipping it to the round top ring. Of course, if you use this method you have to change the lead when you change sides.

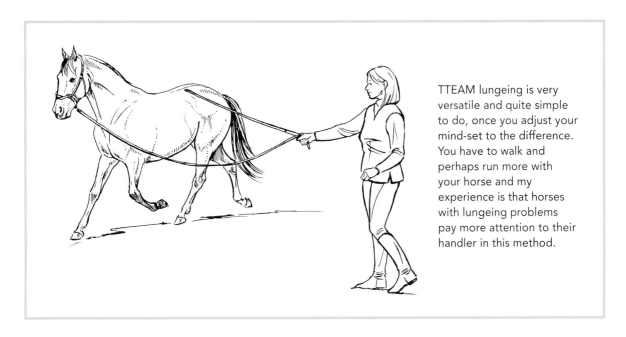

TTEAM lungeing is very versatile and quite simple to do, once you adjust your mind-set to the difference. You have to walk and perhaps run more with your horse and my experience is that horses with lungeing problems pay more attention to their handler in this method.

The Tellington Zephyr lead, made of soft rope. Start by threading the clip through a side dee of the headcollar, passing the rope over the nose and, depending on its length, wrapping it round the noseband once.

Then pass the clip through the other side dee and up the side of the horse's face, clipping it to the top headcollar ring. To change rein, you have to change the rope to fit the other way.

Lungeing with two reins

A progression from single-rein lungeing is lungeing with two reins. For this, you will need to tack up your horse in a saddle with stirrups, or a driving roller. I must stress again that this equipment must be comfortable for the horse, its fit and adjustment being explained in the next chapter.

You can use a pair of lungeing reins and a lungeing cavesson using the two side rings or, for the more advanced handler, lunge from a bridle and bit. Again, for warming up, the horse should be free from training aids or 'gadgets'. Run the outside rein from the cavesson's outside ring, through the outside ring on the roller (use the lowest one to encourage the horse to hold his head down and stretch forwards) or through the stirrup iron (the stirrups being let down to about the bottom of the saddle flaps). The stirrups should be tied together under the horse's breastbone to stop them swinging around and to help keep the reins under better control. You can use a length of binder twine for this, or a stirrup leather of just the right length so that there is no flapping end which could hit the backs of the horse's forearms and irritate or even frighten him. The outside rein passes round the horse's thighs (so first make sure he is accustomed to the feel of a rein here) to your hand, and the inside one can come either directly from the inside cavesson ring to your hand or pass first through the ring on the roller (or the inside stirrup).

The advantage of two-rein lungeing is that the outside rein gives you control of the horse's shoulder and quarters, so encouraging better posture and work. You will need to practise handling the two reins and, maybe, holding a whip at the same time, but it is worth it. Practise with your teacher or with a knowledgeable, sensible friend at first.

This is two-rein lungeing with a roller. The outside rein passes from the cavesson, through a ring on the roller and round the horse's thighs, while the inside one passes directly to the trainer's hand.

Two-rein lungeing using a saddle. The stirrups are down and tied together under the girth area. Again, the outside rein passes from the cavesson, through the outside/ right stirrup, round the thighs to the trainer's hand and the inside/ left one passes from the cavesson directly to the trainer's hand.

Long-reining

From two-rein lungeing it is a small step to long-reining your horse. This allows for better control than lungeing and, although you need to be fitter and more agile to do it – like leading actively in hand – it is more versatile than lungeing and, again, not that difficult to pick up on a basic level with a little expert guidance. You use the same equipment as for two-rein lungeing. You may or may not need a whip of whatever kind is comfortable to hold. A full-length lungeing whip with thong and lash can be difficult for a novice to manipulate and I find a white schooling whip (my Tellington wand) or a buggy whip just as good.

You can walk behind your horse (at a distance comfortable to you and depending on whether or not your horse kicks) or slightly to one side (again, obedience to voice commands is important) and start off in the now familiar long, low and loose walk. Do not restrict the horse: you will have to keep up with him in walk and trot and let him stretch out to loosen and limber up his joints and soft tissues. You can easily change direction by means of a gentle tweak of the inside rein and moving towards that side, supporting with the outside rein pressed against the horse's side. You can also teach him left and right by saying the words as he changes.

You can easily progress to long-reining from two-rein lungeing; just pass the inside rein through one of the rings on the roller. This horse is being long-reined from the bridle but you can use a lungeing cavesson if you prefer.

Long-reining as a system is capable of taking horses right up to high-school work and you may get hooked on it. For now, its uses are that it is easier and less hassle to change direction than when lungeing; you can teach the horse to flex to the rein, as under saddle; you can do some lateral work to start the horse using the outside and inside muscles of his legs, hindquarters and chest and you can perform a variety of movements such as loops, serpentines and figures of eight. Long-reining is excellent for starting off youngsters and showing them around the area as you have good control and can go out of the manège, around the yard and fields and even on quiet lanes, roads and tracks when the horse is used to it and amenable to both the system and your vocal aids.

Long-reining also supples (loosens) up a horse more than the other in-hand methods if it is done well.

Whether you lead in hand at walk and trot, lunge or long-rein, you need about fifteen to twenty minutes to warm up your horse. Finish with some relaxed walking, head down and striding out.

Pole work

Whether leading in hand, lungeing or long-reining, once you have done his suppling exercises and the horse has been led in hand, lunged or long-reined in walk, trot and maybe canter for ten minutes or so, you can do some work over poles for added benefit. This gets the horse to exaggerate his action a little (lift his legs a little higher, push off a little more strongly) and also lower his head a little more to use his eyes to watch where he is going, and think about his gait. Encourage him to keep his rhythm and to refrain from jumping – particularly a full line of six poles, which is far from unknown!

Start off with a single pole and progress to three or four, or up to six when your horse is used to them. Make sure that you know your horse's comfortable walk and trot strides and, if you intend to canter through poles, his canter strides, too. Generally, and depending on the horse, I've found the distances listed below suitable, but it is always important to watch each horse carefully to see what suits him best, and to be mindful of what you are trying to achieve by your spacing of poles.

- A walk stride distance between two poles is about 0.75 m (2 ft 6 in), which is a short human stride or about three of your foot lengths. (It may be a little longer for some horses.)

- A trot stride distance between two poles is about 1.20 m (4 ft), which is a long human stride. (Again, perhaps a little longer in some cases.)

■ A canter stride distance between two poles is about 3.3 m (11 ft), which is about three comfortable human strides.

Remember, you are warming up, not schooling as such. Keep things calm, short and sweet.

Start off with the poles flat on the ground, then, for increased effect, raise one end of each, maybe placing it on the perimeter board of the school. Next, if you have safe equipment such as plastic or wooden blocks of any kind, raise the other ends a little – say 10 cm (4 in) – just to get a little more effort. You can create patterns with the poles to get your horse turning, such as a maze of some kind through and over which you can work him. (For a maze, place the poles about two human strides apart.) Slightly raised poles carefully spaced and radiating out on a circle are also good.

Another interest for the horse, and a means of developing his flexibility and attention, is for you to create obstacle courses to long-rein your horse around, using poles, cones, upturned tubs or buckets, bales or any other safe equipment you have to hand. This will enhance his co-operation, co-ordination and general way of going, if you do it so that he is carrying himself in a correct but relaxed manner.

Working in hand

Another alternative is to work your horse in hand in the classical way once he is suppled and limbered up. This is simpler than you may think, basic work being quite attainable with a little practice. Its advantage is that the horse can start to really use his muscles without carrying weight. You can do this work with just a bridle and schooling whip. Work from both sides in walk to get him carrying himself, flexing his neck and spine not only laterally but also longitudinally. You need to encourage him to tilt his pelvis/hindquarters under a little and bring his hind legs under and stepping well forwards, as in riding, by using gentle taps where your legs would go, or on the hindquarters or hind legs if he is not respond-ing to that. Depending on the height of the horse, the whip can also be used on the side away from you for extra direction or control. (On the understanding that many readers may not be familiar with in-hand work, these processes are explained in more detail on pages 83–87.)

Here again, obedience to the vocal commands is a great help. He needs to understand 'walk on', 'stand' or whatever word you use for halt, 'back' and 'over'. It also helps to have him understanding some encouraging, livening-up sound such as tongue clicks in case he is a little lazy or unsure.

You hold the reins in one hand and the schooling whip in the other. There are two main ways to hold the reins.

1. With the reins on his neck as for riding (see illustration) stand on, say, his left side and hold them about 15 cm (6 in) from his lower jaw. The 'spare end' is obviously over the horse's neck: depending on the length of the reins, you may wish to knot them above the withers. With this method of holding the reins, you can 'feel' either rein separately by squeezing the appropriate fingers or by turning the hand and wrist so that you create a feel more on one rein than the other. You can also move your hand towards his right or his left.

2. The second method gives you more control but some people find it a little harder to master. (However, anything new or different feels strange at first, from driving a car to learning a language, and you simply practise until you get used to it.) The reins are over the horse's neck as for riding. Bring the right

Method 1
This way of holding the reins is a very simple in-hand version of how you hold the reins when riding. You cannot use a schooling whip for guidance and instruction effectively with this method so it is not good for horses who keep stopping, unless they go forward willingly from the voice. It is useful when getting used to working, as opposed to just leading, your horse from the ground. You can obtain poll and jaw flexions by gentle 'feels' on the reins, raise and lower the head, halt up to the bridle, turn and so on, getting him used to gentle but confident bit instructions and to your verbal commands. Keeping one hand under his neck (left or right depending on which side you are working from) you can progress to method 2, holding the reins in one hand and using the other to guide and instruct your horse with a schooling whip.

rein over the neck to the left side and hold both reins on that side in front of the horse's left shoulder just below the withers. Separate them between your fingers as shown below. This second method gives you the definite advantage of a controlling outside rein on the neck – a very effective, classical aid for turning and for controlling the shoulder.

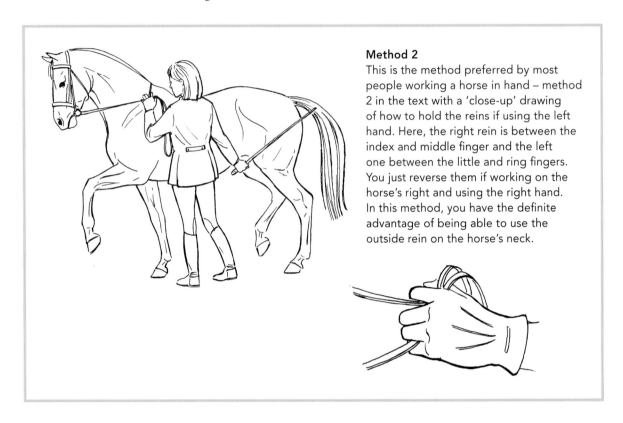

Method 2
This is the method preferred by most people working a horse in hand – method 2 in the text with a 'close-up' drawing of how to hold the reins if using the left hand. Here, the right rein is between the index and middle finger and the left one between the little and ring fingers. You just reverse them if working on the horse's right and using the right hand. In this method, you have the definite advantage of being able to use the outside rein on the horse's neck.

This kind of in-hand work enables you to 'gather' your horse, if not actually collect him, to a degree dependent on your experience and skill, and to perform some lateral work such as shoulder-in on straight lines, around bends and on circles. (Of course, it is also possible to do this work on long-reins but some people find in-hand work easier. Try both and see which you prefer.)

With your horse standing to attention, the reins sorted and your whip in your free hand to act as your 'legs', stand at an angle to your horse's shoulder. You do have to walk a little sideways in this work. Take a *gentle* feel on the bit and stroke your horse's quarters with the whip, lightly but not so much that you tickle and irritate him, at which he would be quite justified in kicking out. Talk to him reassuringly and praise him for acceptance. Stroke down his hind legs and tail and where your legs would go if riding. If he is small enough, pass your arm over his back and stroke his outside shoulder, side and flank.

Now, look to the front, lighten the contact and then give the command to 'walk on'. Expect an instant response, taking a step yourself and watching the horse. If he seems unsure, stop and repeat this familiar vocal aid in a calm, positive tone, immediately followed by a tap with the whip on his side, where your leg would be. Walk yourself, and he is almost sure to go with you *provided* that you do not prevent free, forward movement by too firm a contact on the bit or by actually pulling backwards on it. This very common error, in both in-hand and ridden work, creates a 'shortened' neck and/or a horse working with his face behind the vertical.

Both these results are not only ugly and incorrect but also uncomfortable, potentially painful, and distressing for the horse. A restricted head and neck prevents his muscles and other structures, not only in the forehand, from working optimally and correctly and, therefore, they actually hamper the warming-up and working-in processes. Also, it has been known for many years (and is confirmed by recent and continuing scientific research), that horses can see only down to the ground and thus not where they are going when the front of the face is behind the vertical. (In some horses, because of the setting of their eyes, and the structure and function of the eyes, this restricted vision may apply even if the face is just on the vertical.) The senses of insecurity and frustration (even fear, in some horses), which being partially blinded must cause, are not conducive to creating a relaxed, willing and supple equine athlete. Any adverse emotion causes muscular tension and stiffness – exactly what we do not want.

Sensitivity is always needed with horses for best results and it is perfectly possible, indeed a requirement of good schooling and riding, to get the horse going from the back end forward to a light, giving but existent contact by adequately engaging the driving force – the hindquarters and hind legs. Pulling the horse's head in (which is destructive, not productive) or holding the reins in a rigid, vice-like grip at such a length that he is denied the use of his head and neck will not achieve our aims of a supple, toned up, freely forward-flowing body.

When trying a new technique (and it is my experience that riders at the level for whom this book is written are not familiar with this type of in-hand work), it is easy to be anxious about getting it right and to feel that you will either lose control of your horse or confuse him. As described above, natural reactions to adverse emotions like this are to tense up and probably grip or pull the reins, effectively preventing the horse from doing what you are asking.

So, keep the contact light and confident, neither wishy-washy nor firm and insensitive, and *release it* a second before you ask him to move. A stroke or tap on the hindquarters or the back of the hind legs should work if the tap on the side did not. Praise him the instant he moves, keep the contact light but guiding and keep up with him. Achieve halt by saying your chosen word and slightly increasing the tension on the reins *without* pulling on them – it is more a feeling of resisting his forward movement than pulling – and by halting yourself. Return to walk and try stroking down the backs of his hind legs to encourage them forward, maybe reinforcing this with a click of your tongue. A tap or two on the hindquarters near the root of the tail also can help. Keep your contact light, elastic and consistent – not hard or rigid – and I am sure you will find that you master this useful technique quicker than you expected.

The next stage, for suppling and educating in-hand, is to try a little simple *lateral work*, shoulder-in being the obvious candidate. The purpose of this is to help bring into action the muscles on the insides and outsides of the horse's forelegs (including the shoulders and chest).

- Walk your horse on the track, with you on his inside, of course. Let's say on the right rein so you are holding the reins as described earlier in your right hand and your schooling whip is in your left hand. Have him in a calm but purposeful walk up to his bit.

- Move yourself a little more into the school so that he has room to bring his inside foreleg just off the outside track and is not blocked by your body.

- At the same time, press the outside rein on the left side of his neck by bringing your hand a little towards you and feeling the inside rein with your right ring finger to ask for slight flexion to the inside. This sounds complicated if you are not used to it but, in practice, it is a simple movement.

- You can reinforce the outside rein aid by putting your left hand over his withers and pressing on the side of them with the whip or with your fingers or knuckles. The command 'over' should be useful as an added reinforcing aid. Nearly all horses will perform a very slight shoulder-in or shoulder-fore movement in response to these aids.

- Repeat on the other rein.

The movement does not have to be technically perfect so long as the forelegs move a little to the inside; the hind legs should remain on their original tracks if the bend is correct. If you are fairly new to this work, this is enough to think about for now. There is much more you can do in hand as you gain expertise.

It is interesting that some horses will imitate someone walking near them on the ground. You could try this with your horse by turning your body away from him in the angle you want for the shoulder-in or shoulder-fore, and walking in the way you want his forelegs to move. You may find it easier to transfer your reins into your outside hand, or just cross your inside arm across your body. Some horses will show interest and co-operation by then performing the shoulder-in or shoulder-fore with no other aid, watching you closely. This technique can be used for many movements.

The instant you get any good response, praise him delightedly.

This can bring the groundwork part of your warm-up to an end and the horse can now be tacked up ready for mounting and work under saddle. The programme described is a fairly full warm-up routine for a day when you have plenty of time and/or the work to come is quite demanding. Even so, you do not have to do all of it and a couple of shorter programmes will be given in the final chapter for when you have less time.

SUMMARY – GROUNDWORK

So far we have covered the following techniques in this order:

1. After the massage techniques and suppling exercises described in the previous chapter, leading in hand again for just a couple of minutes allows the horse can get used to the feel of his body after the exercises and the sense of being 'freed up' after using his muscles during a journey or standing in a stable.

2. Lungeing and/or long-reining to bring in trot and maybe canter to get his heart and lungs working more and his muscles responding to more demands in an unrestricted way and without the effort of weight-carrying. He must work at controlled speeds and not be allowed to buck and kick in case of injury. On no account lunge the horse on small circles, particularly at fast speeds as these can be very difficult for him from the viewpoint of balance and force him to use his body incorrectly. Two-rein lungeing encourages the horse to adapt his body more along to line of his circle. Pole work can be included to enhance these effects.

3. Long-reining is more energetic for you than lungeing, but more versatile and starts to get the horse going in a correct outline and in good balance if done properly.

4. Working in hand comes next, if you wish, to start to 'gather' the horse and bring him into hand, his hindquarters and legs coming more under him, engaging and carrying more weight (particularly useful if you have not long-reined him).

CHAPTER 7

Tack and its fitting

After the routine described in the previous two chapters, the horse is ready for ridden work, but first we need to think about the horse's tack and the effects it can have on his mind and body, for better or for worse – and, therefore, on how effective this programme is going to be. These effects depend not only on how the tack is fitted, but also how it is adjusted – it is essential that a horse is comfortable in his tack, not least because otherwise his mind will be on his discomfort, not his work.

Even if everything is the right size for him, if it is adjusted so that it is uncomfortable, restrictive, distressing or even painful he will move poorly and wrongly, with tension and stiffness in his muscles and putting stress on unaccustomed and inappropriate muscles and other tissues. This is called 'compensatory movement' because the horse is compensating for not being able to use the correct muscles properly. Not only will this cause development of the 'wrong' muscles; the horse will also tire quickly and even suffer strain and possible injury, and develop habitual, stiffness, unnatural action and lack of mobility.

Mentally, he will be unhappy and even distressed, which will destroy his goodwill, any pleasure he took in his work and his trust in his rider and/or whoever tacks him up. Working a horse in this state clearly does not benefit either his body or his mind and it is very unfair to him.

Depending on his temperament, a horse in such circumstances may learn to control himself and try stoically to do what is required in the face of such opposition, or he may react by playing up and, understandably, trying to avoid the situation, at the very least by resisting his rider. This is exactly the opposite to what we must aim for in a relaxed, supple, warmed-up athlete ready, willing and able to do his best work and, we hope, enjoying it as much as we do.

No true lover of horses would want their horse to be distressed, of course, but I find that many people, at all levels, often do not seem to fully realize or understand the effects that inappropriately fitted and used tack can have on a horse. Fashions seem to take hold very quickly in the horse world and many people do not question them, so it is a good idea, at this point before the riding stage of our warm-up programme, to look into the importance of the correct fit and adjustment of tack, for the benefit of the horses who have to work in it. (I am assuming that the basics of good fit are understood by readers.)

Tack for groundwork

For warm-up lungeing, this can consist of a well-fitting lungeing cavesson or a bridle, with the addition of a saddle and stirrups or a driving roller for two-rein lungeing and for long-reining. Work in hand requires only a bridle. The fitting and adjustment of the saddle, girth and bridle are detailed further on.

The best type of lungeing cavesson is still, in my experience, the strong, stable leather type with a metal nosepiece, padded and covered with leather – softer leather on the inside where it rests on the nose and stronger leather on the outside where the metal fittings are attached. It should have one ring on a swivel on the front for a lungeing rein and a ring at each side for other items, in our case the reins needed for two-rein lungeing or long-reining. Sylvia Stanier, author of *The Art of Lungeing* and *The Art of Long Reining* (see Further Reading), prefers to have the rings moved behind the cheekpieces for long-reining: I also find that they do give a more direct feel set here, and do not catch on the sides of the nosepiece.

- Fit the nosepiece so that it is not tight, but snug enough so that it does not twist or slide round on the head, pulling the outside cheekpiece with it, possibly on to the horse's outside eye. It must be low enough to avoid rubbing the facial bones and come well above the corners of the lips. It must rest on the bony part of the face, not the cartilaginous part lower down.

- The cheekpieces need to be well back from the eyes.

- The headpiece must not rub or cut into the base of the ears, and must be adjusted so that it holds up the nosepiece in the correct place.

- The jowl strap and throatlatch should be just tight enough to keep the cavesson straight on the head whilst being comfortable. The throatlatch must not come up into the curve of the throat as this will certainly discourage the horse from flexing his head and neck freely and could also cause discomfort.

■ I prefer the lungeing rein to be fairly lightweight as the heavy ones inevitably exert too much pull on the centre ring.

The bridle and bit

Whatever type of bridle and bit you are using, the general principles remain the same. There must be no excessive tightness, no rubbing and nothing touching or catching anywhere that will annoy the horse or cause discomfort or pain, otherwise he will not be happy in his work or be able to do his best.

Bridle

Bridles should be put on and removed with care and consideration for the horse during this inevitably slightly uncomfortable process.

■ The throatlatch should fall about halfway down the horse's round jawbones, so that you can fit the width of your hand sideways between the jawbone and the strap. If it is tighter, the horse will be aware of it even if it does not actually touch his throat, and this can be enough to prevent some horses flexing to the bit willingly, or feeling free to hold and move the head and neck naturally.

■ A noseband ought to be unnecessary on a well-schooled horse with a sufficiently skilled rider for the sport involved! The original design and purpose of a basic cavesson noseband was to enable a standing martingale or tie-down to be fitted – the first step in strapping a horse down. For appearance's sake, many people riding English-style feel that a horse looks unfinished without one. Whatever type you use, the golden rule, so often ignored these days, is that you must be able to slide a finger *easily* under *every part* of it, including over the top of the nose (see photo) as well as under the jaw, around the bit and behind the chin. If you cannot do this, the noseband is too tight and the horse *will* be in more or less discomfort. Also, he will not be able to flex or 'give' to the bit by relaxing his jaw – in other words, by opening his mouth just a little so that he can comfortably accept, feel and lightly play with and respond to the bit. This necessity is stipulated by all traditional standards of good horsemanship, whatever the discipline, but it is clearly not possible if his mouth is strapped tightly shut. The noseband must also not interfere in any way with the horse's breathing by restricting, even slightly, the nasal airways up the face, because horses cannot breathe through their mouths.

A comfortably fitted noseband, allowing the horse to flex his lower jaw to the bit. Although the author would like it a little lower, it is not rubbing up against the horse's facial bones and will cause him no distress.

Bit

The correct, comfortable and, therefore, humane way to fit the bit and adjust its placing is also crucially important. Here again, if we keep to traditional standards we won't go far wrong. These standards were devised by concerned, knowledgeable horsemen for the effectiveness of the bit's action and the comfort of the horse.

The inside of the horse's mouth should be studied by a knowledgeable person such as a vet, equine dental technician or equine management expert with a real feel for horses, because the position of the teeth (the premolars and, in a male horse, the canines or tushes) can affect the height at which the bit is set in the horse's mouth. The ideal place for the bit to lie is across the diastema or bars of the mouth (the part of the gums where there are no teeth, inside the corners of the lips). Whatever the thickness of the horse's tongue, it will more or less fill the mouth space anyway, but some regard should certainly be given to this as different horses prefer thicker or thinner mouthpieces.

At the time of writing, the prevalent fashion is to fit bits too high, sometimes much too high. This is very uncomfortable and even painful for the horse (as a teacher of mine used to say: 'Try doing it to yourself and see how you like it.') Stretching the skin at the corners of the lips in an inevitably constant pressure means that, even without any contact on it, the bit is giving the horse a constant 'stop' aid, which is not what we want. Also, it can cause numbness and even tearing and splitting of the tissues which, in turn, can cause nerve injury and callousing of the area, leading to loss of sensitivity. All this is obviously contrary to what we want and to good horsemanship. The correct standards for the fitting and adjustment of bits are as follows.

HEIGHT ADJUSTMENT

The correct height of different bits is as follows:

- A jointed mouthpiece should create *one* wrinkle at the corner of the mouth – only one. This includes single-jointed snaffles and double-jointed snaffles with a link or lozenge between them, also the bridoon of a double bridle.

- A half-moon/mullen mouthpiece or a straight-bar bit such as a ported mouthpiece, when used alone as in, for instance, a snaffle, a pelham or a Kimblewick, should fit snugly up to the corners of the mouth but create *no* wrinkles.

- The curb bit of a double bridle should lie about 1.25 cm (½ in) below the bridoon (which should be fitted as above), not touching the corners of the mouth at all, and the bridoon must lie on top of it in the mouth.

CURB CHAIN AND BIT

- Curb chains (whatever they are made of) need to lie well down and flat into the chin groove below the jaw for best effect and for comfort: if they ride up higher they can easily rub the thin skin on the lower jawbones and do not work so well. (Be careful with covers and lipstraps: in practice, they can often actually interfere with the action of the chain, so I do not use them myself.) Note that the reason why the chin groove is often called the curb groove is because it is where the curb chain should go.

- The cheeks of a curb bit or pelham should come back to a 45° angle with the line of the horse's lips (or *slightly* less) before the chain comes into effect, so the chain should be adjusted to enable this. The curb rein was devised to be used gently and the fitting described allows the rider to do this without pulling. It is no kindness to the horse to adjust the chain looser so that the bit

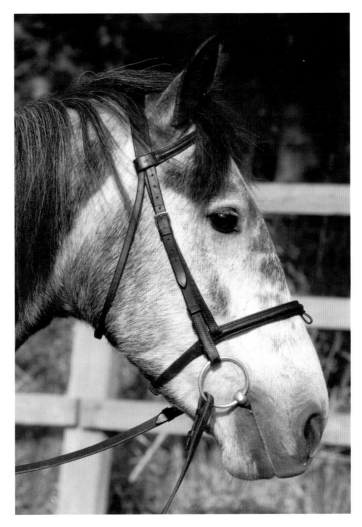

Smokey models a bit at a comfortable height, just causing a slight wrinkle at the corners of her mouth.

cheeks have to come back further before he feels an active contact on the chain/curb bit, because this often moves the bit more in the mouth (which may be uncomfortable and interfere with the bridoon), increases poll pressure from the curb headstall via its cheekpieces and can have the disastrous effect of the rider actually pulling on the curb rein.

The saddle

The saddle is the only item of your equipment that has to fit both you and your horse at the same time. This is not easy if you and your horse are not quite complementary in size and shape. More problems are caused by riders being big for their horses than the other way round. Today, the issue of fit is complicated by the wide range of saddle types available. Whatever design of saddle you require for whatever discipline, there are, fortunately, basic rules of fit to help you find the right saddle for both of you.

I think that far more riding and behavioural problems under saddle are caused by badly fitting saddles than is generally realized. Saddles that do not fit the rider will make it difficult to ride well because they will be uncomfortable. Those that are the wrong design for the chosen equestrian discipline will also make it difficult or impossible for the rider to sit in good balance for that discipline and ride well. Saddles that do not fit the horse cause discomfort and very often pain, so the horse, understandably, expresses this in the only way he can by moving poorly (exhibiting the restricted, changed or compensatory movement, described earlier), by not co-operating, or even reacting downright violently if the pain is severe.

It is easy (and a common error) to think that, because the saddle seems to have plenty of padding under the seat in the panel – which lies (presses) on the horse's back – it must be quite comfortable for the horse, but this is by no means necessarily so. Padding can, itself, be the problem if there is too little or too much, if it is hard or lumpy, or inappropriately distributed within the panels. Deeply gusseted panels commonly cause pressure at the back. The main aspect of fit and design depends on the tree (framework) on which the saddle is built. (There are half-tree and treeless saddles, which can obviate problems of a too-narrow or too-wide tree but, like any product, they have their denigrators and enthusiasts.) You want your horse to move freely, confidently and as naturally as possible under your combined weight of saddle and rider, and the fit and design of the saddle must permit this.

Fit for rider

It is certainly important that the saddle fits the rider, in terms of comfort, balance and effective application of the aids. However, fit for the rider should not *take precedence* over fit for the horse.

Design-wise, the saddle should have its deepest point in the centre of the seat and it is in this dip that the rider's seat bones should sit naturally. For good riding in balance, it is essential that you sit on your seat bones rather than back on your buttocks, which puts too much weight on the wrong part of the horse's back.

The saddle flaps and lower panels (under your legs) must be the right length for you and the knee rolls, if present, must be in the right place for your knees to fit comfortably behind and into them. Your knees must not come forward off the flap or be unable to reach the rolls when your stirrup leathers are an appropriate length.

Placement on horse

Before we can talk about correct saddle fit for the horse, we need to consider correct saddle *placement*, because a saddle that fits comfortably when in the right place can cause all sorts of problems when placed wrongly.

PLACEMENT TOO FAR FORWARD

It is extremely common for saddles to be placed too far forward. This may be because we believe that we must sit just behind the withers for the horse to be able to carry us easily. With most horses, there is a point to which we can carefully slide the saddle back (having put it on just over the withers) where it finds its own place, which will be correct if the saddle fits the horse and is well designed and balanced. Putting the saddle too far forward causes a lot of problems:

1. It can tilt the saddle upwards in front and downwards at the back, constantly sliding the rider back and down towards the cantle, onto the buttocks, putting too much weight on the back of the saddle and disturbing correct balance. This also concentrates the weight on to a comparatively small area of the horse's back, intensifying pressure, instead of its being spread evenly along the muscles of the back. This discomfort causes the horse to go with a dipped instead of an arched back, so up goes the head and out go the hind legs – exactly the opposite of what you want.

2. Because the stirrup bars are then angled instead of horizontal to the ground, the rider's legs and feet are pulled forwards by the stirrup leathers so they are no longer perpendicularly beneath the seat in a correctly balanced position and the whole riding position/seat is well out of balance, making good riding extremely difficult. Sitting with the buttocks on the back of the saddle, as described above, also causes this fault.

3. The saddle also interferes with the free movement of the horse's shoulders and, therefore, his whole action, because of the way the shoulder-blades move. The shoulder-blade rotates around a point about a third of the way down its length from the top, by the withers. Every time the horse puts his foreleg forwards, the top of that shoulder moves back and pushes into the front of the saddle causing discomfort, possibly bruising, and making the saddle rock slightly from side to side with every step. This rocking is not only another discomfort for the horse but further unbalances the rider, this time from side to side.

4. If the saddle is so far forward that the tree points (the bottoms of the front arch just in front of the stirrup bars) actually come into contact with the tops of the shoulders, the discomfort for the horse can become very significant.

5. The girth is unavoidably pulled forwards into the backs of the elbows. This is particularly uncomfortable for the horse because when each foreleg goes back at the end of a stride the front edge of the girth will dig in behind the elbows. This alone is enough to effectively prevent him reaching out with his forelegs and shoulders and moving freely.

PLACEMENT TOO FAR BACK

If a saddle is placed too far back:

1. The rider will be sitting well behind the horse's centre of balance. Looking at your horse from the side, his centre of balance is about two-thirds of the way down his ribcage, inside his chest, about a full hand's width behind his elbow. The key to good, balanced riding is to keep your centre of balance, which is inside your abdomen just below your navel, as close as possible to that of your horse as much of the time as possible. Altering your balance, though, is an extremely influential signal (intentional or otherwise) to the horse, who will adjust his own balance naturally to try to stay under yours, often needing the freedom of his head and neck in order to do so, particularly at speed.

2. Sitting significantly behind the centre of balance often causes the rider to lean instinctively forwards and place the elbows and hands too far forwards, which unbalances and weakens the seat when riding on the flat.

3. Placing the saddle too far back can mean that the panels under the cantle will be pressing on the area above the horse's loins, which is an area to be treated with gentle respect because the kidneys and adrenal glands are here, even though they are well protected by cushions of fat.

CORRECT PLACEMENT

The correct place for the saddle to sit is in that natural position to which it can be slid back from the withers, coming to rest in its own spot, on any horse or pony with reasonable conformation. When correctly placed, you should be able to fit the outside edge of your hand easily between the front edge of the saddle and the back of the top part of the horse's shoulder-blade which extends up to just behind the withers. This will give room for that area to move backwards in motion without the horse expecting or experiencing uncomfortable pressure there. At the back,

Good placement of the saddle, behind the tops of the shoulder-blades and so not restricting them in movement. Also, this brings the girth back to a comfortable distance behind the elbow, thereby preventing it from digging in behind the elbow when the horse brings his foreleg back.

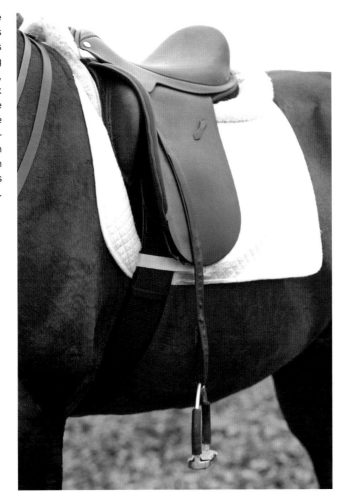

the cantle should come no further back than your horse's last rib, which you should be able to feel along his side. It should not, of course, press on his loins.

POINTS TO CHECK

Other basic points for the correct, comfortable fit of saddle for the horse are:

- The saddle should not touch the spine anywhere at all when the horse's heaviest rider is riding him. You should be able to see a clear tunnel of daylight down the spine under the saddle gullet.

- The saddle should be the right width for the horse. It should not rock from side to side when girthed up, which would probably mean it is too wide. It should also not be too tight anywhere; you should be able to slide the flat of your fingers under the saddle all round fairly easily. I find that common faults with fit today are that the saddle is too tight in front and presses into the back under the cantle.

- Slide your fingers along under the panel and note whether it is easier to do this in the middle than at the front and back. If it is, the saddle is 'bridging' on the back. This means that the panels under the seat are too flat for the shape of the horse's back and it is concentrating pressure at the front and back, with less in the middle. This is a common and significant fault which must be put right.

Check your horse's back when you remove the saddle. There should be no sign of rubbed or, worse, broken hair which means that the saddle is rubbing and maybe pressing in that area. Note, also, whether the flesh appears to have been pressed down anywhere. If, after removing the saddle, your horse develops a lump or lumps on his back, this can be a sign that the saddle is exerting too much pressure in that spot. (Examine the girth area, too, for signs of pressure, rubbing or areas of soreness.)

If you are experiencing problems with fit, simply putting a selection of numnahs and pads underneath the saddle will not solve the problems and could make them worse. Putting anything under the saddle will take up room between it and the horse, making the saddle feel tighter. It is rather like putting on thicker or extra socks inside shoes which are rubbing; they take up room, make the shoes tighter and exacerbate the problem. Rather than doing this, do not delay in consulting a qualified saddle fitter, where available, who holds the qualifications offered in the UK by the British Equestrian Trade Association and the Society of Master Saddlers.

If, subject to informed advice, you do use a numnah or pad of any kind, make sure that it provides a smooth surface for your horse's back with no ridges, uncomfortable seams, stitching or binding which could cause pressure or friction. Make sure that a numnah is big enough for bound edges to come outside the saddle area, otherwise they will cause uncomfortable pressure. Make sure, also, that it is not folded or wrinkled under the saddle for the same reason. Check that it is pulled well up into the saddle gullet by holding the numnah at the front and back and pulling it up, with the saddle a little too far forward and not girthed up. Then, still holding the numnah up, slide the saddle into place to smooth the hair comfortably. Then girth up as normal.

Choice and fitting of girth

The girth should fit a good hand's width behind the point of the elbow to give adequate clearance of the elbows for comfort and unrestricted movement. It always helps if your horse has a natural slight girth groove on his breastbone as this holds the girth, and the saddle, in the right place. Such horses are said to be able to 'carry a saddle'.

There are various designs of girth which are shaped or cut away behind the elbow, and these are very well worth having. Just make sure to measure your horse so that you get the right length and the shaping is in the right area for your horse.

It is a big advantage in comfort for the girth to have elastic inserts at *both* ends for even expansion, or a single one in the middle. Look carefully, though, at how these are fixed on to the girth: there must be no uncomfortable ridges or stitching which could rub the horse sore. A single elastic insert at one end, which is very common, means that the girth only 'gives' at that one end when the horse breathes in, so the saddle will move over to the other side, where there is no give, with every breath, moving back again when the horse breathes out. This will cause constant sideways movement on the back.

Tightening the girth should be done carefully and slowly. *Many* horses resent this process because they are, or have been in the past, girthed up too quickly and too tightly. Your girth should be long enough so that you can fasten it loosely at first so that it just touches the horse. Then apply other items of tack between taking it up a hole at a time until it is just tight enough to keep the saddle on whilst you mount.

Before you do so, carefully lift each foreleg *from the knee*, not the fetlock, and encourage the horse to extend it and his shoulder forward *slightly* to smooth out any wrinkles in the skin under the girth – which might otherwise pinch and cause soreness. This process is often overdone. Many people try to pick up the leg from the fetlock and pull it out straight as far as they can. This is very uncomfortable for the horse because horses cannot lift their forelegs when straight but have to bend them at the knee and then straighten them. Also, it can create too much stretch in the leg and injure tissues. The object is only to smooth out the area under the girth without pulling the skin uncomfortably far forward.

Always try to mount from a mounting block or something similar which is safe, even if you are quite fit and agile enough to mount from the ground – and ideally try to do so by swinging your leg over the saddle without putting your other foot in the stirrup. This prevents uneven pressure being put on one side of the saddle and, therefore, on your horse's back, and also stops sideways tension on the girth, both of which make the process uncomfortable for him. Vaulting on is the next best thing, provided *the vault* is your main means of mounting – not hauling yourself up by the saddle!

After riding for about ten minutes, you will of course need to check the girth. Over-tight girths, even with elastic inserts in them, cause a lot of discomfort and certainly discourage, or even prevent, the horse from breathing freely, which must be a horrible feeling for him. Remember that the girth goes round his ribcage, which has to expand during breathing. A reasonable guide to adequate tightness is that, when you tighten the girth from the saddle after riding for some minutes, you should be able to fit the flat of your fingers between it and the horse without being able to pull it away from his side. Girths which are too loose, of course, may not do their job of securing the saddle and can rub and irritate the horse.

Driving rollers

Many of the comments about saddles and girths apply also to driving rollers – they must not be too far forward, because they will dig in behind the elbows, or too tight, in which case they will cause discomfort. Many people like to use a breastgirth and/or a crupper to keep rollers in place but if they fit and the horse has reasonable conformation they are not essential.

Other tack

As mentioned earlier, I am not in favour of any other tack for warming up except leg protection such as tendon boots, specific support boots, brushing or speedi-cut boots and overreach/bell boots.

Some people still prefer to bandage the legs instead of fitting boots and this is fine provided the bandages are put on expertly with just enough pressure to keep the padding in place. A very great deal of harm can be done by over-tight band-ages, even over padding: circulation can be interfered with, tissue seriously damaged, pain and discomfort caused and the action of the leg hampered. Band-ages put on too loosely are dangerous as they can unravel and trip the horse. If bandages are applied under the fetlock to aid support (still a moot point) remem-ber to leave them well up at the front so as not to interfere with the flexion of the joint or cause pain from pressure across the front of the joint when it flexes.

If you are not an expert at bandaging, remember that experts were not always experts either. They had to learn and so can you. You can practise on a table leg at first, then on a patient, co-operative horse in the stable. Have a lesson from your teacher, if you like, but do not be persuaded to bandage tightly. If you use stretch bandages *do not* pull them much at all as you apply them because they have a self-tightening effect and can easily become too tight.

Whatever leg protection you decide to use, it must cause no discomfort to the horse and must be of definite help.

SUMMARY – TACKING UP

Tack up your horse so that he is truly comfortable in his tack, otherwise he will not only be distracted, thinking of his discomfort, but will probably use his body incorrectly as he tries to compensate for the discomfort, or even pain. Correct fit is important but so is correct adjustment. Making a horse wear tack which causes pain or discomfort is also contrary to his welfare.

PART **2**

Under saddle

CHAPTER 8

Warming up

At last you are in the saddle! Depending on what you are planning to do (active, athletic work or something less demanding) and how much warming up you did on the ground, the mounted warming up and more demanding working-in stage will take from ten to twenty minutes or so.

Your horse will be pretty well warmed up if you have done all, most, or at least some of the things detailed earlier, but he must now use his muscles for carrying weight and adjusting his balance whilst doing so, and must pay attention to what you are asking plus (with respect to his survival mechanism) what is going on around him.

Weather conditions

Horses, like us, warm up more slowly in cold weather, so make allowances for this and take longer. Some people like to take a horse pretty soon into a slow, loose trot in cold weather (after a couple of circuits in walk), to warm him up more quickly, but if you do this be sure that the trot *is* slow for several minutes. Energetic trotting, gymnastic work or trying too soon to get the horse into 'an outline', 'on the bit' or 'in the frame' (whatever term you use) – even when you know how to do this correctly – can cause muscle and other soft tissue or joint injuries. This is particularly so in any situation in which the horse's muscles are actually tense, such as when he is cold, excited, frightened and so on. Forcing them to work significantly in that state is asking for trouble.

Horses are like people in that some are sensitive to the weather and do not work at their best in conditions they find stressful. Many horses, I find, hate hot summer weather and, of course, the flies and midges it brings, but most also dislike wind and rain, especially if they have to face into it. Of course, it is not always possible to let the weather dictate your exercise plans if, for instance, you are at a competition, an organized ride, hunting, or doing some other event, but take steps to protect your horse from extremes of weather at all times.

It is quite possible in warm or hot weather (especially if he has travelled to his venue or has been in a small, stuffy showground stable) that he could be over-heated even before he starts work, so it is very important to check his tempera-ture at least and to keep him in conditions as cool as you can find. He also needs to have water freely available until about half an hour before starting strenuous work; less for moderate or light work.

If he does have to stand around in unpleasant conditions, try to find some shade for him and a breeze in summer, or let him stand with his tail to the wind and rain in inclement weather, ideally with a rug over his back and down his tail. If he gets either overheated or chilled, his work performance will be affected but, more importantly, his welfare and possibly his health will suffer, so think in terms of consideration for him.

Working a clipped or sensitive horse in an exercise/quarter sheet in chilly weather can be a good idea. There are different designs and materials from natural wool to acrylic, polyester and other fabrics. In wet weather, a showerproof or waterproof sheet should be used, as others become soaked and heavy and make the horse cold and miserable rather than allowing him to warm up properly. Take care over its fitting. A common mistake is to use a sheet that is too short. The muscle mass area of the hindquarters is a vital part of the horse's 'engine' and needs to be warm to work properly, yet so many quarter and exercise sheets stop short at the croup. Your horse's sheet should go right back to the root of his tail and the best have shaping there to lessen the amount of wind and rain which can get underneath the sheet. An essential piece of equipment is a fillet string around the horse's thighs under his tail to stop the sheet being blown up by the wind.

The first few minutes

Your horse will be completely aware of your mental and physical state and if you are tense or distracted, in a hurry, on edge or nervous, he could well take his cue from you. You absolutely must try to calm down and concentrate on your horse in a happier, more relaxed way. Legs clamped on, a clenched seat and an unre-lenting grip on the reins are all guaranteed to upset your lines of communication with him and hype him up or cause resistances or lack of confidence in you.

Breathing in rhythm with your horse's gait or, if you can sense it, his own breathing, helps the link between the two of you and also helps you to be calmer and more tuned in to him. In canter, anyway, his breathing is tied in to his gait – he must breathe in time with his footfalls, breathing out as the legs land and in during the moment of suspension. If you practise yoga or Pilates you will understand the effect on your own body of different breathing techniques. So far as riding is concerned, making a point of breathing out in a relaxed way is a calming signal to your horse, and taking an inward breath can be used to slow down or halt, or as a call to attention.

Whether you are working in a manège, out in the country, going for a hack or working-in at a competition venue, the first few minutes should, if at all possible, be spent at a walk on a completely free, loose rein. This will enable the horse to feel his balance and swing along with all his muscles working naturally, alternating between contracting and relaxing, and loosening up his whole body. This is important to allow the free circulation of blood, lymph and energy.

The difference between a free, loose rein and a merely long one must be appreciated. The purpose of very free, unconstrained movement is to allow the soft tissues to work in a loose, flexible way which allows the blood, lymph and energy to flow freely through the muscles, the joints to move naturally and stimulate the production of more synovia (joint oil) and the tendons, ligaments and other tissues to limber up. Bringing a horse into the manège and making him work 'in an outline' quickly or even immediately is asking too much too soon and does not allow the tissues and body structure to be properly prepared for work, or safeguard them adequately against injury.

As discussed in Chapter 7, working a horse who has not been properly warmed up can also encourage compensatory movement as he tries to avoid discomfort caused by stiffness: he moves in an unnatural way, which can damage tissues and joints. Even on a long, as opposed to a loose rein, the horse is under a controlling influence on his head and neck and, therefore, his whole body, and he will not move completely freely, so the warm-up will not be so effective.

When horses are brought into 'an outline' too early in the warm-up or, worse, *held* that way at any time, the muscles of the neck and shoulders in particular (although this adversely affects the whole horse) do not get enough opportunity to alternately contract and relax, pumping fluids through their tissues with their ready supply of nutrients and oxygen and removing carbon dioxide. When muscles are contracted they are shortened and feel harder, and it is not so easy for fluid to pass through them. In this state, too, they are working and producing carbon dioxide, which needs to be removed by a free flowing of blood. There needs to be plenty of opportunity for relaxation, and for the horse to stretch out and swing along in a long outline to prepare his muscles and other structures properly for work.

The only times when giving a horse a loose, free rein may not be appropriate are when the horse is likely to shy or jump about if he is in an exciting or strange place or surrounded by strange horses, or if he is fresh from lack of exercise. Even accepting that riding is a risk sport, safety (and therefore control) are always paramount so you may naturally feel that you don't want to give him his head just yet. In such circumstances, give him as much rein as you feel is wise whilst still retaining a 'reminding' contact if he is likely to do anything other than walk calmly or at least obediently, lengthening it as soon as you feel able to do so. It is always a good idea to teach such horses to direct their energies into their work from the outset: contrary to popular opinion, they should not be allowed to play about to 'get it out of their system' either under saddle or during groundwork, as this can cause injury to unprepared tissues. Instead, they should be ridden with a contact just sufficiently firm to give control until they have settled and can accept a free, loose rein.

A greenish horse not yet in self-balance under a rider will also need some support, from the outside rein – the master rein – in particular, but not to the extent of pressurizing him into any particular kind of shape. He may also not be ready for the canter work detailed later in this chapter.

For a fairly experienced horse, used to a systematic warm-up routine and to co-operating with his rider, an ideal warm-up under saddle initially consists of him calmly walking, trotting and cantering on straight lines and large circles for about ten minutes in horizontal balance on a completely loose rein. The poll should be about level with the withers, and the muzzle in front of a vertical line when the horse is seen from the side. At this stage, he is still warming up, not yet working in.

Thinking about the aids

Guide the horse's gait and direction with a light seat, weight and legs, using your mind and eyes to signal to the horse and show him where to go, maybe supporting these aids with an open inside rein and/or the outside rein or hand pressed lightly on the neck just in front of the withers to assist turning. *Where you put your weight, and where you look, your horse will almost always go* unless you prevent him by, for instance, unintentionally giving a contrary rein aid, or unless his attention is riveted elsewhere.

Let's discuss these techniques a little more because they are invaluable in all riding, taking the emphasis off the head and the hands and placing it on the mind and the seat. For warming up on a loose rein, they allow you to keep your balance and direct your horse easily and with little physical work on your part, which can only make life simpler for you and your horse, and achieve the results you want with the least effort.

Consider that the busier the rider, the more tense the horse is likely to be. It is not true that 'the rider needs to be doing something at every stride'. If the horse is doing what you want there is no need for you to do anything. Physically, tension causes his muscles to clamp up, thus losing the essential loose, free movement we need, and mentally the horse becomes pressurized, anxious, irritated and stressed as he tries to cope with the constantly changing and often contrary messages flooding in from his rider.

Weight aids

Weight or seat aids are one of your natural aids, the other ones being your voice, your hands and your legs. To these we should add your mind (thinking in pictures to your horse can be really effective) and your eyes (concepts explained in the next sections of this chapter).

To apply weight aids, you use your seat and your legs. It is important to understand that weight aids rely on the fact that the horse wants to stay in balance. If you carry a heavy backpack and it flops around from side to side you instinctively move to the side where its weight is to rebalance it and yourself. However, as a rider, you do not wish to seem to the horse like a randomly moving weight: instead, the aim is to use controlled adjustments of weight in a subtle manner.

The pathway to riding with subtlety and finesse and getting maximal results from minimal aids is to learn to balance on and ride from your seat bones (those two areas on the lowest part of your pelvis), not your buttocks. To do this successfully, you need to be able to completely relax and loosen the muscles of your seat and legs as if you had no use in them – at least until you get the hang of it.

Just sit up straight, stretching up from the waist with shoulders back and down, being careful not to hollow your back. Completely loosen your seat and leg muscles and drop everything down from the waist, draping your seat and legs lightly down and around your horse. It is easier to do this without stirrups at first: be sure to let your toes hang naturally downwards because keeping them up creates muscular tension and stiffness. Once you are sitting upright with your lower body loose, feel for your seat bones immediately under your body and sit lightly and quietly on them. A good, balanced seat like this is closer to standing up than to sitting down.

You will probably be familiar with the traditional, correct seat. From the side, an observer should be able to 'see' a vertical line running from your ear, down through your shoulder and hip and on down the back of your heel. (Once you get used to habitually maintaining this position, you will find it even easier to balance if you carry your feet just a little further back so that the line runs through your ankle bone because this joint, not your heel, is the point of flexion in your ankle where any concussion is absorbed.) Your upper arms should drop naturally straight downwards so that your elbows are held lightly but definitely on your hips, not inches in front of them, which can encourage your upper body to slouch forwards. You may need to lengthen your reins a good deal to permit this and to allow the horse the freedom of his head and neck for warming up.

Now that you can feel your seat bones, ask your horse to walk in a straight line on a loose rein: give a quick squeeze inwards, not backwards, with your legs. Ask him to turn, say to the right, by putting your right seat bone a fraction forwards and sitting just a little heavier on it, at the same time looking with your eyes (not turning your head) where you want to go and imagining both of you going there. Do not give a rein aid. If you do this correctly your horse *will* turn right like an old hand. This is because this aid applies the principles of nature to direct your horse, and your horse became an expert at that a few days after he was born.

If you find it tricky (because it is unfamiliar) to actually move or weight your seat bone, just put a little more weight down your right leg (without tilting your body over sideways) by pressing your right heel down so that there is more weight in your right stirrup. It's rather like stretching your leg down. This will have the same effect. Be careful not to let the foot and leg move forwards out of position when you do this, so that you keep your balanced seat.

Practise this around the manège in walk until you get used to it, asking your horse to walk out freely on a truly loose rein. With practice, you can easily transfer the technique to sitting and rising trots and to canter.

The mind as an aid

I am sure from observing horses together that they can communicate with each other by using visual pictures. They try it on us but often give up because we do not habitually use this technique and so they usually get no response. If you are open to this idea and start to use it, I am certain you will find that it works, whether from the saddle or on the ground. It is important to keep it a two-way communication: try to discern what your horse is sending you (you don't have to be looking at him) and make your imagined pictures to him clear and positive.

Visual aids

Using your eyes as an aid sounds unlikely. How can the horse know where you are looking if you use no other aid, and why should he take it as a direction?

A member of the Equine Behaviour Forum wrote a contribution in its members' journal, *Equine Behaviour*, which pointed out that if the horse is slightly flexed in the direction in which you want to go, you will just be able to see from the saddle the corner of his eye. This is the traditional criterion for judging the right amount of flexion. We know that horses have almost all-round vision and that they are extremely visually perceptive, noting the tiniest movement or even nuance of demeanour in other horses and animals, including people, as well as changes in their environment. The author of this contribution suggested that the horse could see out of the corner of his eye his rider's eyes and thus where his rider was looking and, therefore, intended to go, so he naturally complied.

My own experience is that this works, even if the eye is obscured by forelock and if the horse is not flexed, but it may be that he is picking up on my mental intention to go in a certain direction.

Both mental and visual aids are well worth trying. Stay calm, quiet in your body and still in your mind, and concentrate. Give them a chance and you should be pleasantly surprised.

Attaining horizontal balance

Even though your horse is warming up on a free rein, it is important to ensure that he does not go on to his forehand or go too fast, which will put him out of balance. This is not good for any kind of riding because it feels horrible to ride a horse in this way and it encourages the horse to lean on the bit rather than taking a light contact, and thus be heavy in the hand. This does not make for a good, educated and light mouth. Also, it puts unnecessary weight on to the forelegs, which can over-stress them long-term in a horse who habitually goes in this way.

But how do you get a horse to go in horizontal balance or slow down if you are using a free rein? You use your seat and upper body positions, and your mind again, to bring his forehand up and towards you a little.

The need for this is more likely to occur in trot, of course, and you will be in a light rising trot for the warm-up. Refine your technique for this by thinking of dropping your legs down all the time and keeping them close to, but not clamped on, the horse's sides. Do not push yourself up and down with your legs. Keep them dropped and *allow* the horse to move your hips forwards, rising as little as possible, and sit straight down afterwards with your bottom tucked slightly under you, so you are going 'forward – sit – forward – sit' with a neat, natural technique that keeps you close to the saddle and makes it easier to balance than in the leg-flapping, thrusting type of rising trot so often seen.

(Remember, the less you do to get the results you want, the easier it is for the horse to detect a real message when you give him one, rather than ignoring the

This drawing has been done from a photo taken by the author of one of her clients. The horse is working in excellent horizontal balance. His back and belly are up, his hindquarters are tilted under and his hind feet stepping well forward. He is voluntarily, slightly stretching his top line by bringing his nose just a touch behind the vertical. More than this is unnecessary. His self-balance is indicated by the loose rein: he could not work in this posture on a loose rein were he not balanced.

'white noise' of constant movements from you, which eventually turns horses off from light aids.)

In this type of rising trot, slightly tone the muscles down your back, hold your upper body and seat up and back a little in the saddle whilst continuing your 'forward – sit'; breathe in and slightly raise your hands. Be sure not to let your feet swing forwards. It is much easier than it reads in print. Think positively of drawing or even sucking the horse's whole forehand up towards you and picture him doing it. If it helps you, go into sitting trot for a few strides. It increases the effect if you temporarily slightly tense the muscles of your seat and thighs, too, as you do this. Also, as you raise your hands, actually turn your wrists so that your fingernails are facing the sky. This combined technique is actually a powerful stopping aid if exaggerated a little more, and always gets a horse to take more weight on his quarters even though you have applied no significant physical force (certainly no pulling on the mouth) and particularly if you stay calm and strong and use your mind and voice as described.

We are not getting into the realms of telepathy here – it really works. It just takes a bit of practice and concentration. By all means use your voice. If he is going too fast, I find a long drawn-out 'easy' in a low, calming tone works well, and think 'very slow' to him, even 'reverse'. A 'we're not going anywhere' attitude helps to calm and slow a horse, but you have to maintain it firmly in your mind no matter how fast he goes. In other words, ignore his speed and concentrate on yours. Slow your own rhythm and think 'slow'. This mental aid and attitude combined with the physical aids just described works with most horses. If you pull on the reins this will create resistance and feelings of competing (with you), also resentment because it is so uncomfortable.

If the horse is simply on the forehand, try saying 'come up' as you raise your hands, sit back a little (it's a lesser version of the above aids) and think to him 'up and back'.

Of course, if you actually need to use light bit contact to achieve this you must do so, because horizontal balance is important. But praise the horse and release the contact, and the other aids, the *instant* you get your result, as this tells him he has responded as you required. (If he then falls on to his forehand again, and/or travels too fast, repeat the whole process immediately.) It really is easier to do in practice than it is to picture when you read about it – and it certainly works.

Movements for warming up

When you first go into the manège or your warm-up/work-in area, keep the movements you ask for large, loose and flowing. I'll imagine you are in a manège preparing for a schooling session or lesson. The principles can be applied just as well in a field, collecting ring or any other warm-up area.

Make a point of doing no more than one circuit of the manège at a time on the track. Nothing is more destructive of interest, willingness, enthusiasm and constructive work than slogging round and round on the outside track, not knowing what to aim for and achieving nothing. A good variation is to walk one circuit on each rein on the outside track to let the horse get a feel of the surface, to know where he is and to see what is on the outside of the manège, or inside it if there any jump stands and so on. (Incidentally, never work your horse on bad surfaces such as those which are too deep – including wet – uneven, too stony or, from trot upwards, too hard. These can not only cause injury but destroy good movement.)

Progress in walk to a couple of figures of eight, guiding your horse with your seat, your mind and your eyes (as described earlier) and, if necessary, an open inside rein and a little pressure on the outside of his neck just in front of the withers with the outside rein or hand.

After this, come on to the inside track and keep walking. This is to prevent the horse from psychologically 'leaning' on the school fence, not keeping himself straight and not listening to your outside aids: it also makes you use the latter to direct your horse. A horse's shoulders are narrower than his hips. When on the outside track next to the fence and *seemingly* straight, many horses are, in practice, going *very* slightly with their quarters in or in a semblance of the movement called *travers*. This is because they naturally line up their outside shoulder and foreleg and their outside hip and hind leg with the fence, so their inside foreleg is placed very slightly out (towards the fence) in comparison with their inside hind leg – in effect, the horse is just a little crooked. Working on the inside track does not have this effect and horses often straighten themselves. If they do not, you can easily get the feel of the two different locations and should soon be able to tell when your horse is going with reference to the fence or working independently of it, and straight.

On the inside track, walk on both reins, then take your horse into a steady, free and loose rising trot. Get him into the habit of going at a moderate tempo (speed) and check any tendency to speed up, charge along or go on the forehand with the hind legs inevitably trailing. Maintaining his horizontal balance, perform figures of eight, changes of rein across the diagonal, shallow loops and large serpentines in that order. Keep your seat light, your movement with him and your lower body muscles just a little toned and controlled, but not at all stiff.

When your horse is used to warming up in this way and can maintain horizontal balance, you can warm up in canter the same way. It is a good plan to use a light or half seat for the canter work, your seat just out of the saddle and your shoulders above your knees. This frees his back and hindquarters and is easier for him. Try to take a good deal of your weight on the inside of your thighs instead of sending it all down into the stirrups, which would increase the pressure on his back just behind the withers where the tree points and stirrup bars are.

Start with just a very few strides and gradually build up, emphasizing the horizontal balance. This may take a few days or, more likely, weeks, depending on your horse's natural balance and his past experience of being ridden. So many horses are used to being held in and up by their riders in the mistaken belief that they are then 'going correctly', whereas they are actually being denied the opportunity to learn to balance themselves under a rider and, consequently, developing the wrong muscles. At this stage, going in any kind of outline approaching being 'on the bit' is not beneficial although, as mentioned, you must take more control by means of rein contact if the horse is playing about.

In this type of canter warm-up, perform changes of direction across the diagonal and ride 20 m circles, and maybe figures of eight based on these big circles with a few trot steps as you change rein (or flying changes if your horse is experienced enough). This is no big deal if you think about how easily horses in self-balance can do them in the field. Their difficulties come when they have to carry a rider who is giving unclear aids or is not in good balance with them and, even then, many agile horses and ponies do change as required, using their own initiative and instinct as to what they need. Although horses at liberty very often rebalance themselves momentarily before making a flying change, being in collection or even on the bit (as commonly understood) is not necessary for flying changes – ask any horse! I may be hauled over the coals for saying this but it is a fact. On the other hand, the experience of riding flying changes using only your seat bones, on a classically trained horse in perfect self-carriage, is one you never forget.

Don't overdo the canter work – you are only warming up. If your horse is not too fit, be sensitive about whether or not you do it at all and, if so, do just a circuit on each rein and maybe one figure of eight if his balance is good enough.

In trot and canter, horses sometimes try to cut corners or to balance themselves if going too fast for the circle or bend requested by using their natural balancing pole – their head and neck – which they turn to the outside of the bend or circle, leading with their inside shoulder and usually tilting inwards – motorbiking or banking – as well. This is not only dangerous (as the horse might fall) but injurious to his body, and it creates the wrong habit and mind-set. Do not let the horse go so fast that this sort of thing starts to happen.

Keep the speed controlled and reasonable but not too slow, either, or you will get an untrue gait and breaks from canter down to trot. Keep the horse out on his bends and circles by putting a little more weight on your outside seat bone and perhaps down your outside leg, *without* tilting outwards or collapsing at the waist to the inside. Just stretch your leg down. The horse's head and neck should correct themselves once the balance and speed are restored but you can help by giving an opening inside rein, holding your inside hand in towards the centre of the circle and, if necessary, vibrating the inside rein gently. (In canter, it often helps the horse to step forward with his inside hind leg – and thus balance himself and keep correct bend – if the rider also provides support from a deep but not weighted inside leg, with the inside seat bone forward.)

After this loose warm-up, walk or stand your horse on his still-loose rein to relax for five minutes or so. His pulse will now be at about 80 bpm and his body ready to start working more gymnastically in the working-in stage.

I realize that you may feel that all this is quite complicated and surely not necessary. In the case of a horse or pony going out for a relaxing hack or a not-too-demanding schooling session or lesson, you can certainly shorten the process considerably. However, if you go to any fairly high-level competition and watch, for example, the way advanced event horses warm up, work in, cool down and finally warm down, you will realize the importance of this kind of preparation (and aftercare) to equine athletes. Remember, also, that although your horse may not be that talented, you may well be asking him to perform at his personal best level which, to him, is just as demanding. In exchange, he deserves that you do justice to his efforts for you, and you will probably find that, being correctly prepared before work and treated after it, he will become a better performer than you ever expected.

SUMMARY – WARMING UP

- Protect your horse during the day by finding shelter for him in wind, rain or hot sun, and covering him with a rug, if necessary. Do your early warm-up in an exercise sheet if it is very cold.

- Keep calm, firm and positive to influence your horse's attitude. Try breathing in rhythm with him to both relax and energize him, and to communicate your 'feel' for him. Walk him for about ten minutes on a completely loose, free rein, having regard for the surroundings and your mutual safety, so that the blood can flow freely and the muscles move naturally.

- Do not let your horse go on his forehand, however, as this stresses the forelegs. Teach your horse to go in horizontal balance during his warm-up.

- Remember: where you put your weight, and where you look, your horse will go.

- At all gaits, ride with as still a seat and body as possible and in the best balance you can achieve, as this enables the horse to work well in balance with you and avoids unnecessary muscle use.

CHAPTER 9

Working in

Working in is the stage of preparation for work in which we ask the horse to come into hand and begin to take up a working posture which is correct (see below) and also appropriate for *him*, taking into account his conformation, natural way of going and level of training. Now that he has warmed up and it is safe to do so, we ask him to use his body more gymnastically, working his soft tissues and joints to develop them and prepare them for the actual work to come.

The fabulous four

There are four things a rider needs to understand before knowing how to work in a horse properly. They are:

1. *How to recognize correct and incorrect movement in a riding horse.* When you are working in, you obviously need to have a clear and correct idea of what you are aiming for, how a riding horse in any discipline should go and how his body will be affected if he does not (or is not allowed to) hold himself and move correctly. There seems to be widespread misunderstanding of these crucial topics, so they should be addressed before we talk about working a horse in. Correct movement develops and enhances a horse's body, action, mind and, it seems to me, his spirit, too. Incorrect movement can do a lot of harm, build up inappropriate muscles even to the point of apparently 'deforming' a horse, stress soft tissues and joints and also distress and upset horses. None of this can be regarded as good horsemanship or humane treatment.

It will help you if you can develop at least a basic eye for good and poor movement, both in other horses and in your own when you are in a position to watch him, such as when you are working him from the ground or when someone else is riding him. You need to be able to recognize both correct and incorrect physical work when, and wherever, you see them so that you can always aim for the former with your own horse and avoid the latter. (This skill is most enlightening and can completely change your outlook on riding. You will be surprised by how critical and what a good judge you become once you have learnt it, and some of your discoveries from your observations of other horse and rider combinations will be real eye-openers!)

2. *How to recognize the feel of a horse going correctly or incorrectly under you.* 'Feel' is the basis of equitation and many people insist that it cannot be learned from a book. This is not entirely true and I hope that I can describe it in such a way that you will know it without doubt when your horse gives it to you. It certainly helps greatly to have a good teacher who understands correct feel and can also recognize it from the ground when observing it in a horse and rider under tuition.

Another huge bonus is to be able to ride at least one accomplished horse who goes correctly, holding himself in self-balance and self-carriage, engaging the muscles and joints of his body so that he habitually goes in the manner described below – or will assume it easily when asked correctly.

3. *How you can affect a horse, for better or for worse, by the way you ride.* A riding horse in any discipline responds not only to what his present rider is doing to him but also to what some other rider or riders in the past have done to him. As a result of his experiences under saddle, he may have developed a faulty way of going because of bad or inappropriate riding which has caused him to move poorly, to develop the wrong musculature and to present evasions out of habit or from expecting his present rider to treat him the same way.

As a classical riding teacher, I find that very many riders are actually taught to take too firm a contact and even to pull in a horse's head and neck and hold them in and up with a rigid, even vice-like grip. This serious and common fault is certainly not described in any of the best literature on equitation, old or new, but somehow appears to have become widespread and its bad effects on horses' development, action, behaviour, attitude and well-being can be seen almost anywhere today.

The opposite end of the scale is having horses ridden with little or no contact. This is far less harmful but will not encourage a horse to adopt the self-controlled, arched, rounded posture and muscular development needed for easier and safer, dynamic weight-carrying. I hope the techniques described below will explain this important issue and help readers to achieve it.

Riding out of balance with the horse also produces uneven muscular development and hampers the horse's balance and agility. Futhermore, tense hips, seat and legs prevent the development of 'feel' in the rider and cause the horse to be tense, too. The ill-effects of tension were described earlier.

Once a horse has learnt how to hold himself and move under weight (which will become easier for him as his muscles develop correctly) he will go in self-balance. This, in turn, will enable him to become agile and light in hand, but he cannot do any of this if he is not ridden with correct understanding and technique.

4. *How to recognize a horse's emotions,* as these betray whether he is working comfortably and correctly or otherwise. You need to be able to understand and accurately identify equine emotions because they will tell you whether or not a horse is going comfortably, co-operatively, calmly and enthusiastically or whether he is distressed, fighting or tolerating discomfort, being coerced or drilled, held forcefully in a particular outline, shape or 'frame', co-operating under duress and with difficulty or (understandably) evading his rider's demands.

Let's look at these four points in turn.

How a riding horse should, and should not, go

We all know that horses were not meant or designed to carry weight, but we sit on them nonetheless. It is generally accepted (by we humans, at least) that a horse should be able to carry about a sixth of his own weight quite easily: some, whom we call 'weight-carriers' and who are usually of a stocky type of build, can carry a bit more than this but others, usually the finer types, can only carry somewhat less than that with ease.

The horse is, in practice, carrying weight already because his heavy internal organs are suspended by soft tissues from the underneath of his spine and the undersides of the tops of the ribs. The spine is naturally slightly arched or bowed, which adds strength to its structure. (Convexly arched bridges, all else being equal, are much stronger than straight ones.) If the horse's spine were not arched, weight-carrying, from underneath or on top, would be more difficult and stressful.

However, when a rider mounts, the spine does sag or dip a little. This has the effect of introducing abnormal stresses on its structures (bending it the wrong way, as it were) and causing the head and neck to rise and the hind legs to trail out behind, if only slightly. In fact, by sitting on him we are making the horse hollow

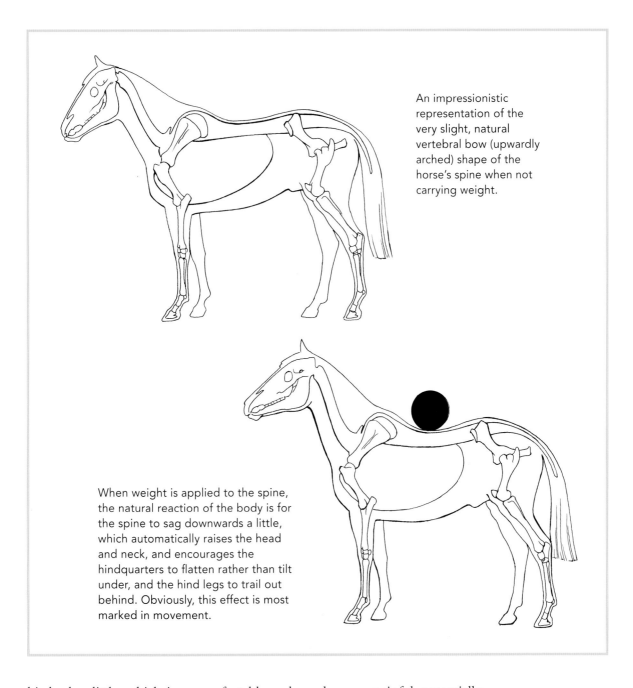

An impressionistic representation of the very slight, natural vertebral bow (upwardly arched) shape of the horse's spine when not carrying weight.

When weight is applied to the spine, the natural reaction of the body is for the spine to sag downwards a little, which automatically raises the head and neck, and encourages the hindquarters to flatten rather than tilt under, and the hind legs to trail out behind. Obviously, this effect is most marked in movement.

his back a little, which is uncomfortable and can become painful, potentially damaging, and is also a weaker posture. The horse cannot thrust so strongly with his hind legs and so his movement is less efficient. The head and neck may even rise beyond the point of comfort and easy control, which does not make for a calm horse or a safe horse/rider pair; furthermore, the bit will not be acting correctly in the mouth, which is not only inefficient but can cause injury and pain.

Very basically, what we need to do as riders is encourage the horse to raise or hump his back a little underneath us to maintain this arched structure – known as the 'vertebral bow' – so that he is better able to carry our weight. This also involves him tucking his hindquarters under a little, and also necessarily his hind legs, these being attached to his pelvis which, in turn, is attached to his spine. Thus the belly is lifted and the head and neck are carried naturally a little lower as well. This posture is:

- Safer for the horse under weight.

- Much more efficient from the aspect of forward movement, as the hind legs can thrust the horse forward more easily (so the horse is 'engaging his hind quarters', 'bringing his hind legs under him' and 'going from behind').

- More stable and exhilarating for the rider.

It also presents a much more pleasing picture to knowledgeable onlookers.

When working in correctly, this posture is exaggerated *slightly* in order to gently but effectively stretch and work the major system of ligaments, muscles and tendons along the horse's top line (his neck, back and hindquarters) to maintain or increase his flexibility and agility. The muscles on what would logically be called his 'bottom line' (but isn't) – those under the lower aspect of his neck, his belly, loins and hindquarters – are also involved as they work to raise the bottom of the neck and thrust the whole neck outwards, to raise the belly, tuck under the horse's hindquarters and bring his hind legs more forward under him with each step. The top line and 'bottom line' muscles together are often referred to as 'the ring of muscles' because we can imagine them going all round the horse when we picture him seen from the side.

The result of 'the ring' being used correctly and beneficially is a stretched, rounded outline with the horse looking long on top and short underneath. Often, unfortunately, the system is not used correctly. The key to making full and *beneficial* use of it is to ask the horse to go with his head and neck low and the front of his face on the vertical or to bring his nose *just very slightly* behind the vertical. These two positions, with the horse flexing a little at the poll, exert a slight, beneficial and safe stretch along the top line ligament system, which is what we need.

If a horse is worked with his head and neck low and stretched out but with the nose poking forwards, and is not asked to flex at the poll and stretch over his top line, he will not raise his back and will not, therefore, develop the physique necessary for weight-carrying with less effort and risk. An experienced equine body-worker, or a trainer with a sound understanding of equine biomechanics can see immediately from a horse's muscle development whether he has been worked

correctly, whether he has been allowed to go 'flat' with no poll flexion and, there-fore, no raised back and tilted pelvis, or whether he has been forced into an exaggerated shape and looks rounded to the uninitiated but is clearly not cor-rectly so to an educated eye.

With horses whose natural conformation is like that of most Thoroughbreds and Arabians, for example, with the front of the face carried naturally well in front of the vertical, I should certainly not ask them to bring the muzzle behind the vertical, but on it. In horses whose natural conformation and carriage is with the front of the face more approaching the vertical, such as most Iberians and similar horses, and many heavier-type horses, bringing the nose just slightly behind the vertical creates enough stretch. And this is only for working in, not the work proper.

The conformation of the horse's throat is also important. For good riding conformation, the traditional standard is that a man should be able to fit his fist between the horse's rounded jawbones, into his jowl. This 'open' throat confor-mation means that the horse should be able to flex easily without cramping up the tissues of his throat area. The throat should form an attractive arch, which must be maintained when the horse is going correctly, pushing his neck and head

Sky and Vicky working in. A good, swinging trot on a rein loose enough to allow Sky to stretch down and encourage his back to lift. His nose is very slightly behind the vertical, which gives that little extra emphasis to the posture and its consequent effects.

121

A horse going freely in trot with his head and neck in a fairly free posture, accepting and going up to his bit, nose just in front of the vertical and with an open, arched throat area – just what to aim for.

In contrast to the drawing above, this horse is being ridden with a harsh, rigid contact and on too short a rein, with the result that his neck is shortened and cramped, his throat area tight and angular and his nose behind the vertical. This will be causing tension and even pain in the muscles of his entire forehand and also his back as he tries to perform whilst also trying to relieve himself of his considerable discomfort.

forward and 'giving' or flexing in the poll and jaw rather than being pulled in and cramped up in the throat. Horses who have a more angular throat conformation have problems flexing because it is uncomfortable, painful or even impossible. If a horse is asked, or forced, to over-flex in terms of his individual conformation, he will be in significant discomfort or even pain in the throat area, will probably have his breathing restricted and will never flow freely forward in comfort and enjoyment of his work. Such horses can still be ridden, of course, and can be very tactfully asked to just give the lower jaw and perhaps flex at the poll only as much

above An Arabian showing the natural throat conformation of most hot-blood breeds, including Thoroughbreds and horses with a lot of Thoroughbred genes.

A Paso Fino, showing the natural throat conformation of Iberian horses and their descendants.

as is comfortable for them. They need to be assessed sensitively in this regard by someone who understands their problem.

Many people today misunderstand the correct working-in technique and the reasons behind it. They make their horses go with their heads much too far behind the vertical, sometimes even with their chins touching their chests and, because they are actually pulling the head in, they shorten and often raise the neck, giving it a 'squashed in', shortened appearance, often with a downward bend in front of the withers. This causes great discomfort for the horse, difficulty in breathing because the windpipe is 'kinked' in the throat area, and causes stress and even pain in the muscles of the neck and forehand. It more or less negates the effect of the hindquarters and legs being asked to tilt under and thrust.

Sometimes horses are made to go with the head and neck very low and, in extreme but not uncommon cases, with the front of the face approaching being horizontal to the ground!

As a shiatsu therapist, I have often come across horses who are very tender in the poll and upper neck area and often in the shoulders. Their riders have all, without exception, told me, on being questioned, that they habitually work their horses well behind the vertical 'to stretch the top line'. This, of course, is greatly overdoing and misusing the technique: it is not only counter-productive but, from my experience as a therapist and classical riding teacher, I believe that it is injurious and, therefore, contrary to horses' welfare.

This horse's face clearly shows distress. The throat area is very cramped, the nose-band obviously very tight and the bit contact harsh to the point of being brutal. The nose being well behind the vertical will also be restricting forward vision.

The fact that some horses bring their heads behind the vertical voluntarily, usually as a means of trying to escape pressure to the mouth, discomfort or pain, is no reason to regard the posture as normal. Common it may be nowadays, probably because of a misunderstanding of the topics discussed above; normal it is not. Horses will adopt this posture when playing, either at liberty or during ground or ridden work, but they only do it in a head-tossing way *for a few moments*. No horse goes with his head well behind the vertical for comparatively extended periods and we certainly should not make them do so.

There is another point to consider in all this: *the horse's eyesight*. We have known for many years, and now have scientific proof of it, that horses cannot see very far in front of them when their heads are carried behind the vertical because of the structure and functioning of their eyes. Causing a horse to carry his head in such an extreme posture is effectively blinding him so far as forward vision is concerned because all he can see is the ground right in front of his front hooves. This surely cannot be condoned on welfare grounds.

So, then, the posture we need during working in is for the horse to be emphasizing his vertebral bow structure, with his hindquarters tilted under and his hind legs being brought well forward under his body, thrusting forward and acting as nature intended – as his power source or 'engine'. Crucially, the horse's neck must be lifting up from its base immediately in front of his shoulders and pushing forwards and down, with his muzzle encouraged by the rider to be on or *just* behind the vertical, depending on the horse's natural head carriage. It is absolutely crucial that the rider not only encourages but allows this by using a light hand on a long rein, with a giving and taking contact, rather than actively preventing it by pulling the head and neck in and/or holding it in rigidly and harshly.

To introduce this kind of work gradually, the poll in a green or young horse can be level with the withers, at the same level as for warming up. The fact of bringing in the muzzle just a little is enough of a stretch at first but, after a very few weeks, depending on the horse's natural conformation, head-carriage and progress, the poll can be encouraged to be held just below the withers. As the horse gains in understanding, strength and balance over a few weeks of tactful, correct work, encourage the poll to be a little lower until it is level with your knee and the muzzle is always on or only just behind the vertical. This is the method used by the best, traditional classical schools to obtain the raised-back, rounded posture and is relevant to all riding horses for the development of strength, agility and independent balance.

In time, from this posture, the horse can retain his arched, rounded outline and the lifted, extended neck as he learns to go in correct collection, if this is your aim. The head and neck are gradually raised (*never* pulled in), so that the horse is lifting, rounding and extending his neck forwards, finding his way 'into your hands', which must allow this gift of his mouth which the horse is offering. The throat will be rounded and open. The front of the face is just on or a little in front of the vertical, depending on his natural carriage and conformation. The well-schooled and well-ridden horse lowers his hindquarters a little in collection, which gives the impression of the forehand being raised. This cannot happen, in fact, but the slightly lowered quarters, the vertebral bow posture, the neck pushed up from its base and arched forward (without being in any way tight or rigid) and the front of the face just in front of the vertical, give the self-controlled, developed, rounded picture of a horse in correct collection.

The ligament down the top of the neck (the nuchal ligament) is very 'stretchable': we all know that horses can bite at a fly on the breastbone between the forelegs with no problem, and scratch their own hips with their teeth. A trained equine bodyworker can perform passive ground exercises to encourage the horse to both lower and raise his head and neck. Passive exercises are those in which we move various parts of the horse's body for him so that he uses no muscular effort himself. Active exercises are those in which he needs to use his muscles to do the movement himself. For example, flexing the head and neck up, down and to both sides can be done by offering the horse his favourite titbit so that he uses his muscles to reach for the treat. Before attempting either passive or active exercises of this sort, ask your therapist to do them and to show you how, because if they are done wrongly the horse could be injured.

Riding technique for balance, lightness and correct development

Many people are of the school of thought that you should not touch a horse's mouth but let him come up 'into hand' in his own time when he is ready. Others believe in the opposite extreme of actually pulling in the horse's head because they think that is how he is supposed to go. As in so much of life, extremes of any system rarely work, and this applies to these two. They both result from lack of knowledge and understanding, or from being misinformed, and I hope that the description given above of how a riding horse should and should not go has clarified matters on this subject.

I stated earlier that I was going assume that the reader's horse was 'reasonably well-schooled'. This obviously presumes that the horse is not young or green, but a few words on such horses will aid understanding. Young or green horses cannot have the muscular development and strength of a seasoned riding horse because they have not done the gymnastic work necessary to reach that state. Therefore, their sessions should be short – even twenty minutes is enough at first – with gymnastic work in *very* short spells (even seconds, sometimes) interspersed with plenty of breaks on a long rein, during which the horse is perhaps being accustomed to other things such as seat aids or, of course, just resting.

Let's take the first of the two examples of extremes given above; that of a horse whose mouth has not been touched. Continuing to ride a horse in this way will eventually show you, by honestly observing the horse's lack of muscular development along his top line, that this system does not work because your horse will always look and go like a plank.

In the second example, the horse ridden on a pulling rein, such horses do develop muscle, but much of it will be built up as a consequence of using the body to resist, fight or compensate for the extreme discomfort and even pain of being 'held in'. The muscles developed are in the wrong places for the posture required for strength, self-balance, agility and safe weight-carrying.

A horse has to be 'mouthed', to use an old term, if he is to accept the bit confidently and willingly as guidance from the rider. 'Mouthed' does not just mean being accustomed to having a bit in his mouth: it means being educated as to its messages, and the horse will not be willing or able to absorb this education if the bit is fitted, adjusted or used in such a way as to cause him discomfort, pain or distress (see Chapter 7).

Our aim is to get the horse working from the hindquarters, thrusting forwards in the 'vertebral bow' posture with all that goes with it, but to encourage the horse to go in this way he first needs to accept the bit, giving to it and flexing slightly at the poll so that he exerts a slight stretch along his top line, bringing his back up, his quarters under and with his neck pushing up and forwards from its base. This is not the same at all as having his head held in firmly, or worse, his neck 'shortened' and, in his efforts to relieve his discomfort, kinked down in front of the withers, or being forced to go in an overbent way. The horse does not, indeed *cannot*, actually give to the bit when ridden in this way. He will also almost certainly go with his back down, which completely negates the whole process.

Many riders seem to find it difficult from the saddle to get the horse to flex willingly at the poll and hold the flexion himself when he subsequently feels the contact lessen. It does require sensitivity, empathy and timing on our part, and practise on the horse's part. The easiest way for you and your horse to achieve the necessary flexion at the poll (between the skull and the first, topmost vertebra in the neck – the atlas) is to start on the ground, somewhere quiet where the horse has no distractions and you can both concentrate for a minute or two, because that is all it takes. Before you start any new work, you should be calm, confident and exuding good feelings towards your horse.

Have your horse tacked up in whatever bridle he will be working in. Breathe in rhythm with him for at least several breaths and stroke his withers and lower neck, speaking quietly to him. Stand close to him with your back to his tail and hold the reins under his neck as if you were riding. Believe it or not, it really influences the horse if you stand in good posture, stretching your spine up, shoulders back and down, and standing with your elbows on your hips in a good riding position. If you are on his left, make the right rein your outside rein. He will be standing naturally on loose reins, so take up a definite but gentle contact on both reins similar to how you would hold the hand of a toddler to take him across a road (enough to control him but not hurt him), or to hold a small bird in your hand to stop it flying away, but without causing it discomfort. Keep this contact still on the outside rein and give soft but definite little squeezes or 'feels' on the horse's mouth with the inside rein, asking him to 'give to the bit'. These should not be jabs but actual squeezes as if you were squeezing out a sponge. Make sure the direction of the squeezes is straight up the rein as if you were riding. Squeeze and release, squeeze and release on the inside rein, all the time maintaining your still contact on the outside rein, and the horse will quickly get the message and flex at the poll.

The *instant* he does so, say a word or make a sound unlike any other you use with him, such as the word 'give', so that he associates the action with the sound. This is so that you can use this word later from the saddle, or in other groundwork such as long-reining, to help obtain flexion. Another very useful command to teach your horse is 'head down', for obvious reasons.

At the same time as flexing at the poll, most horses will also correctly relax the lower jaw (open the mouth very slightly) by opening the joint just below the ear where the lower jaw joins the skull – the temporo-mandibular. This is exactly what the educated horseman wants because it enables the horse to accept comfortably and play lightly with the bit, keeping his mouth responsive and promoting feather-light, two-way communication between horse and rider. Needless to say, the noseband must be loose enough to allow this, being adjusted as described in Chapter 7. It is essential that you keep your hands still and light, *not taking the contact backwards*, because the horse has flexed as required to your squeezes and lightened the pressure himself. If you then bring your hands backwards with his lower jaw to keep the previous weight of contact, he will not feel any release of pressure (because there will be none) and will not learn that flexing stops it, or that you are asking for that particular movement (flexion). Instead, he will become confused, less than happy and confident in you, and will never attain a light, made mouth.

With riders unfamiliar with (a) this technique and (b) the feel of a horse who is light in hand, they usually comment that the horse has come 'behind the bit' or 'behind the contact'. In fact, the horse has simply *lightened* the contact

Here Pat and Smokey, a Connemara mare, demonstrate a pony going calmly, comfortably and well on a light rein, in self-balance, back raised, neck stretched up and forward from the shoulders and presenting an altogether happier and more correct picture than that in the photo on page 124.

by softening (flexing) at the poll and the jaw, so that he is accepting your now comfortable communicating contact rather than tolerating or even fighting the previously heavier, oppressive one.

Once your horse has flexed to your inside rein pulses, drop the reins, stroke him and repeat. Then do the same on the other side. Take him to a couple of different areas on the yard and perform the flexions once on each side in each place. This makes sure that the horse does not come to associate this little exercise with just one place, but can transfer it anywhere. Then do it whilst you are walking along, on both sides, and remembering to always keep your hands still when he has complied. Once he has clearly got the hang of it, he is ready for you to ask him the same thing from the saddle.

Mount the horse, do your warm-up, short or longer depending on what you are planning to do and how much time you have, stand or walk around on a free rein to relax him and let him get his breath, and then begin working in.

Use the same technique just described to obtain flexion at the poll. If you have done your introduction on the ground correctly you should not have any problem. If you do, get a sensible friend to walk alongside and give the squeezes on the inside rein, because having someone on the ground next to him giving this aid will now be familiar to the horse and he will flex. If you are not familiar with this work, it would help to have an observer on the ground, anyway, to tell you how the horse looks and to ensure that you do not bring him behind, or too far behind, the vertical, because it is very easy to overdo it with some sensitive, willing horses. Start this work in walk and get the feel of riding with light hands and reins (also loose, still seat and legs), with the horse in the correct working-in posture. Progress to trot, using the same techniques on your part and the same posture on your horse's, and, as you both become used to this, move on to canter.

The fact that your horse has responded to your requests to lighten up and not lean at all on your hands means that he is working in self-balance. Do not confuse this with going behind the bit or overbending as an 'evasion'. Self-balance is the start of self-carriage in collection on the weight of the rein alone. Remember that you still *have* contact on your light rein because the horse can feel, and will now respond to, the slightest movement of it – a vibration, a swing, a move to the inside to invite him round a bend without pulling him into it – all the time maintaining his posture. Self-balance on a light rein in correct posture is what working in is all about. It develops the horse's physique, his balance, his agility, his responses, his initiative (because he is not struggling against the restraint of being held in an uncomfortable and incorrect posture), and it improves his trust in you, and your mutual relationship.

At first, the horse will not be physically capable of maintaining this working-in posture for more than a few strides at a time. Try to make sure, though, that it is you and not he who initiates the rest and relaxation periods, so that he does not develop the habit of giving up and only working when *he* decides to. You need sensitivity to learn when he is finding it hard work and needs a rest, as opposed to those times when he just does not want to work. You also need to learn to work out *why* he does not want to work, because it is wrong to work a horse who is feeling off-colour or is in some kind of pain or discomfort.

You always have to have psychological, as well as physical, give and take. Your horse needs to trust you and know that you will not distress him. I believe that horses also need to know that we care about them – so send him this message freely.

Drilling a horse for too long causes distress and physical pain. In the early stages, if you get three or four strides in the correct posture as described, be very happy, relax and stroke your horse. Very gradually build up or repeat these in one session, a couple of times on each rein, then stop. Your horse will gradually build up the muscles and other tissues needed for an adequate work-in if you ask regularly but for very short spells, both in the manège and out hacking or elsewhere.

At all times when warming up and working in, do not confuse speed with free, forward movement or impulsion. Speed excites some horses and is not the same at all as gymnastic work. The horse must be moving comfortably, willingly and enthusiastically forwards but well within himself, maintaining self-balance and with no tendency to lean on your hand. He cannot do this if he is going too fast.

Although you use your leg aids to activate the hindquarters and hind legs, do not make the common mistake of using them at every stride. Achieve the required posture of the horse and the desired level of impulsion, then stop the leg aids, keeping your seat and legs soft and adapting them to the movements of his back and sides. This is for the same reason as keeping your hands still and neutral after obtaining flexion of the poll and jaw – if you do not stop the pressure (psychological or physical) once you have obtained what you are asking for, the horse will never learn the correct response (because whatever he does doesn't relieve him) and he is well on the way to becoming 'dead to the leg', as we say.

Once you've got what you want, there is no point in keeping asking for it. Enjoy it for the few strides you will get initially and stop asking for it before the horse stops giving it. Let him relax, then ask again. Always be very sure that you are not asking for too much. You should be able to feel when he needs to rest. Always build up gradually. Working in is hard, gymnastic, physical effort and it does not need to last longer than about ten or twenty minutes, depending on the horse and your aims. He has already warmed up, after all. It is counter-productive to cause the horse to work in a prescribed posture for the whole of the working-in session because this will cause muscular pain and subsequent stiffness and these will sicken the horse. He will learn and develop more quickly if you keep things short and sweet, working for a few seconds to a very few minutes, then having a relaxing stretch and a walk, or standing still, before working again.

Recognizing and understanding 'feel'

It is not everybody's privilege to be able to learn 'feel' on a truly correctly educated schoolmaster horse, not least because they are getting rarer as riding schools close down (at least in the UK). Not all training yards allow students or clients to ride their best horses, yet the old rule was always that the fully trained horses taught the novice riders and the educated, competent riders taught the green horses. In some establishments this does still happen and it is well worth looking at adverts, listening to word of mouth, visiting a few websites and ringing round to try to find a place that is willing to teach you this way. I suggest that you look for one that teaches classical riding because the way of going described in this book is fundamental to correct classical practice and effective working in.

When a horse is going in the posture I have described above, the feeling you get is unforgettable and really exhilarating, the more so if you yourself have developed it. It has been given various descriptions. I describe it as a power-boat feeling, with all the energy and power coming from underneath and *behind* your seat as the horse thrusts forwards from his back end and seems to lift his forehand lightly into your hands. This feels like a forward and upward force, almost like energy travelling along a diagonal line from the ground (the horse's hind feet), pushing you forward and up with it.

Another way in which I could describe the feeling is as being like a powerful sports car with power steering, which lifts up and pushes you back in your seat when you put your foot down. It has also been likened to sitting on the crest of a wave that is surging towards the beach, lifting you up and forwards effortlessly. It is definitely a 'pushing forwards from behind' feeling rather than a 'pulling forwards from in front' one and it gives you a real thrill.

The light forehand is an inescapable result of this hindquarter-surge and correctly rounded posture, because it is impossible for the horse to lean on your hands if he is lowering and using his hindquarters properly and you are not holding him in or up. Gentle, accepting – even questing – contact is one thing; being heavy in hand is quite another.

The feelings you get when this is not working are quite the opposite. Instead of the behind-and-up feeling you get a forward-and-down feeling – and not a pleasant one at that. Many people, when working horses 'long and low', experience this but seem to think that this is what to expect when the horse is working that way. But the forward-and-down feeling indicates that the horse:

- is not lowering his hindquarters;

- is not raising his back;

- is not in self-balance;

- is carrying too much weight on his forehand and, therefore, his forelegs;

- is using the rider, via the bit, to steady himself and therefore

- is not developing the correct muscles and balance to make work easy for himself and his rider.

A clear example of a horse not in self-balance. Neither rider nor horse looks comfortable or happy.

Long and low is fine for working in if the horse is in horizontal balance. How to achieve this was described earlier. Therefore the correct and beneficial long and low posture *still involves the vertebral bow, with the horse tilting his bottom under and bringing his hind legs beneath him for powerful, contained thrust.* The rider gently but positively controls the energy coming forwards by means of light hands on the reins, in particular the outside rein, not letting the head go *too* low, and maintains horizontal balance mainly with the seat.

The feelings you will get when a horse is going poorly underneath you are, variously, a downward, sinking feeling beneath your seat and thighs, a demanding contact as the horse leans on the bit because he is not balancing himself, the feeling of the hindquarters *rising* behind you and a feeling of being pulled forwards and down into the ground.

Horses who have never been ridden and worked correctly (whatever age they are) may, indeed, lean on the bit but, by working first for horizontal balance and then self-balance, their way of going can always be improved provided they have reasonably good conformation. Sometimes, too, a change to a bit with a different action from the one the horse is used to can work wonders. The proviso is that the rider realizes that the bit is only an *adjunct* to good riding, the main basis of which is a seat that is independent of the reins and adapts, by its movements, to the movements of the horse's back – which leads to the rider communicating with the horse mainly through the seat rather than the hands.

Recognizing horses' emotions

Horses are very sensitive animals both physically and psychologically (or emotionally). This may be hard to credit with certain individuals but generally it is true. Their bodily demeanours and facial expressions speak volumes but, whereas the rider receives information about a horse's emotions by means of feel, an observer receives it by means of body language and the look around a horse's face and head.

Learning to really understand what you are looking at can tell you whether or not a horse is comfortable, enthusiastic, willing, co-operative and happy to be doing his work or is distressed, worried, anxious, really upset or even in a state of physical or mental torture. It is an excellent plan to start looking closely at horse and rider combinations at any equestrian event you attend and to look beneath the superficial picture they present. If a horse is clearly not happy, it is most likely to be the way in which he is being ridden or worked from the ground that is causing his problem. Sensitivity towards and empathy with horses comes more easily to some people than others, but if you think that you are not too good at assessing horses in this way, you can make a good start by learning to understand body language and looking at horses in a completely open-minded, non-judgemental way, so that what is really happening in front of you is not masked by your pre-conceived ideas. Learning to feel horses' emotions is just as valuable as picking them up by visual observation.

A horse's overall body picture tells a lot. What you want to see (and feel) is a horse with a noticeably calm atmosphere about him. He should carry himself confidently and have a rounded flow about his action. His back should swing, not be as stiff as a sideboard, and his dock should swing with it. If it doesn't, there is stiffness and tension somewhere. Remembering the correct, rounded posture we have been discussing, see how many horses really match this picture, going with their forelegs arching and reaching out, rather than flicking forwards with up-turned toes, and moving their thighs and shoulders freely forwards and backwards rather than simply moving their legs from stifle and elbow.

Which part of the horse is your eye drawn to? That is where there will be some problem.

Does the horse's head-carriage look voluntarily and freely assumed, with his face in front of the vertical and his throat curved and open, the rider clearly on a light rein, or is he obviously being pulled and held in, with a stiff, tight and

This horse looks to the author as though he is actually in pain. His misery shows plainly on his face; he is extremely uncomfortable in the mouth, fighting the hard contact of the bit and frothing excessively, which is a sign of distress.

unmoving head and neck in a shortened profile, and creases in his throat area and maybe in front of the withers where the neck is kinking downwards? Are there copious amounts of froth and saliva around his mouth, maybe even splashing on to his forehand and forelegs? If so, contrary to popular belief, the horse is in more or less distress, probably in his mouth, because excessive salivation is a sign of distress in mammals. The mouth should be slightly moist, not lathered up.

Does the horse give the impression of having a flattened or even sagging back, with his hind legs not coming under him but trailing out behind, and is he plainly working too fast and struggling to balance? Depending on the type of work involved, *excessive* sweating, raised blood vessels under the skin and flaring nostrils can indicate that the horse is being ridden too harshly, certainly so if accom-panied by a wide, worried or frightened look in the eyes. You would expect these signs (other than the eyes) in fast work, but not otherwise. It is true that gymnastic work necessitates effort, but certainly not to the extent of the horse looking upset, wet through and overworked.

Riding in this kind of posture will not in any way develop the horse's physique beneficially – very much the opposite.

Finally, looking at his head and face; do you see a confident, interested and basically calm expression, especially in the eyes, even through any excitement? The ears should be flicking around, taking in information from round about, or flicking towards the rider or handler as signs of attention. Tight skin and chin, nostrils wrinkled up, dull, closed eyes or, conversely, wide, anxious ones, and ears stiff and back are all signs of tension, anxiety and unhappiness. Grinding the teeth is a definite sign of distress and discomfort, not merely 'a habit', as it may be described.

These are just some pointers to help you recognize how the horses you are watching are feeling and, therefore, whether or not they are happy in their work – and if not, why not. If you see these signs in your own horse but have not recognized them before, or other people have passed them off to you as normal and showing that a horse is 'working properly', try to work out the causes (with sympathetic help, if necessary) and put things right.

Exercises for working in

The working-in stage, as we have seen, involves getting the horse working more gymnastically to develop his muscles and other structures and thereby to make him stronger, more agile, more responsive and a pleasure to ride.

General school movements and figures

In addition to doing your normal walk, trot and canter work in the posture explained in the previous chapter, this stage can also incorporate transitions from one gait to another (including correct halts) and variations within the gaits – that is, lengthening and shortening the stride as, for example, changes between a working gait and its medium form.

Vary your patterns and exercises to use different muscle groups and keep your horse alert to the work. Apart from circles (at whatever size he can do comfortably), use deep and shallow loops, serpentines, spirals down from a 20 m circle to whatever he can do – say 15 m or 10 m if he is quite supple and balanced. Figures of eight involving two circles are a traditional exercise, but using also triangular figures of eight (see diagram) brings in a different dimension which involves transitions down from trot or canter so that he can negotiate the sharp corners. These can be walked around, or you can perform turns on the haunches in each corner. The transitions, rounding the corners in walk and the turns on the haunches all help to engage the hindquarters and hind legs and lighten the forehand – provided you do them properly, not pulling him around by the mouth, of course.

Lateral work

Lateral work, even the beginnings of it, comes into the working-in stage as it supples the horse and works muscles and joints; it also develops and strengthens the muscles on the insides and outsides of the horse's legs, from knee and hock all the way up to shoulder and hip, and creates a well-rounded, versatile athlete.

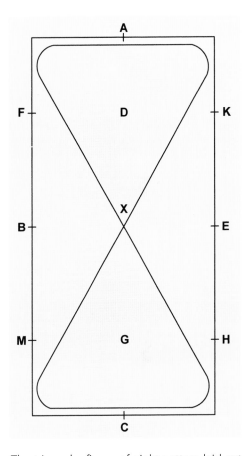

The triangular figure-of-eight pattern laid out in a manège. This is a very useful exercise and can be performed in walk, trot or canter according to the horse's needs and capabilities. It offers opportunities for straight lines; curves; lengthened and shortened strides; turns on the haunches in the corners; simple lateral exercises such as shoulder-in around the corners and down the short sides; frequent transitions to balance the horse, engage his hindquarters, command his attention and make him more supple, agile and co-operative.

TURN ON THE FOREHAND

To establish obedience to the leg and develop the muscles of the thighs and hindquarters, turns on, or about, the forehand are effective but they should not be used much because they do put the horse's weight forward on to the forehand to free the hind legs so that they can move over. To do a beneficial turn on the forehand, without necessarily aiming for high precision, have the horse standing to attention in good posture and (to turn to the right), flex his head and neck slightly to the right so that you can just see the corner of his right eye, looking yourself towards where he is now looking. Then put your right leg back from the hip and, without raising your knee or heel, push sideways with it intermittently against his side, asking the right hind to cross over in front of the left and then push out to the right as the left leg lifts and moves left.

A quarter-circle is enough unless the horse is capable of doing a half-circle correctly. Repeat in the other direction, reversing the aids. Don't ask for more than he can do and always praise instantly.

Pauline and Waverhead Rose demonstrate a turn on/about the forehand, which is the first step towards lateral work and teaches response to the leg aids. There is a little too much flexion in the neck but Rose is stepping well across with her inside hind.

TURN ON THE HAUNCHES

Turns on the haunches bring the weight back on to the hindquarters and develop the muscles of the forearms, chest and shoulders.

- Again, have the horse standing correctly (or walking, if you wish to ride a walk pirouette).

- To turn his forehand to the right, slightly flex his head and neck to the right so that you can just see the corner of his right eye and look to where he is now looking.

- Put your right seat bone forward a little and put a little weight down your inside (right) leg into your heel.

- Your outside (left) leg should be back a little from the hip against his side, to stop his quarters moving left (and it might help to have your schooling whip in that hand).

- Keeping your elbow bent and at your hip, move your right hand to the right to invite him to turn and press intermittently with your outside (left) rein sideways against the neck just in front of the withers. This should result in him moving his forehand to the right, but you may need to give a nudge or two with your inside (right) leg just behind the girth to generate energy.

- Repeat in the other direction, reversing the aids.

Depending on the horse's competence, don't ask for too much, and praise quickly.

INTRODUCING OTHER LATERAL EXERCISES IN WALK

Other basic lateral movements for strengthening and physical development are leg-yielding, also shoulder-in and shoulder-out on straight lines and curves. From the viewpoint of muscular development and working in, these movements are easiest for the rider in walk as there is time to think, but easier for the horse in trot as he has the impetus of the gait to help him. This gait also improves his agility. In walk, his muscles are entirely responsible for moving him and so work harder.

LEG-YIELDING

Leg-yielding is performed on straight lines, often from the manège quarter line to the track or from the centre line to the quarter line or, if the horse can do it, all the way from the centre line to the track. In leg-yielding, the horse looks away from the direction of movement. The main problem riders have with it is that the horse simply goes on a diagonal line to the track and does not cross his legs. This is because the rider has not used enough inside leg to move the hind legs and quarters over, or enough outside rein to stop the shoulder leading towards the track.

Remember – where you put your weight and where you look, your horse will go.

To perform leg-yielding, you can start by just doing it from the inside track to the outside track, which will take only one or two steps. The horse should be used to turns on the forehand and haunches and thus to moving sideways from the leg.

- Have your horse in a good walk with a normal, gentle contact on, say, the left rein on the inside track.

- Flex him a little to the left, so that he is looking away from the required direction of movement.

- Look to the track (your right) and put a little weight on your right seat bone and down your right leg (at the girth to help prevent the shoulder leading).

- Press your outside (right) rein firmly sideways against the horse's neck just in front of the withers (which is your main aid to stop the shoulder leading).

- Your inside (left) leg, applied behind the girth to move the quarters right, taps or squeezes on and off, to ask the horse to cross his legs and go to the track. (As the horse will probably be used to the verbal command 'over' to move him over in the stable, you can use it now to augment your total aids.)

- Repeat on the other rein, reversing the aids.

Build up to leg-yielding from the quarter line to the track, from the centre line to the track and also from quarter and centre lines to each other – which makes you use your leg aids and weight properly to control the direction and stop the horse simply falling towards the fence. Don't ask for too much too soon.

SHOULDER-IN

Shoulder-in is a brilliant all-round suppling, strengthening and balancing exercise and, contrary to common belief, is not an advanced movement but a basic schooling technique and wonderful for working in.

In *shoulder-in on a straight line*, the horse is flexed away from his direction of movement, carrying his shoulders into the school a little off the outside track. The exercise can begin with a very slight version called *shoulder-fore* (see diagram) in which the inside shoulder/forehand is brought only about a hoof's width off the outside track. For our purposes here, the object is simply to have the horse bent a

This diagram illustrates the very slight amount of lateral movement asked for in shoulder-fore, a useful and subtle forerunner to shoulder-in used to introduce horses to the idea of it. The outside fore steps only slightly in from the outside hind, not even in front of the inside hind as it would in a three-track shoulder-in, and the inside fore is just a little to the inside of the inside hind.

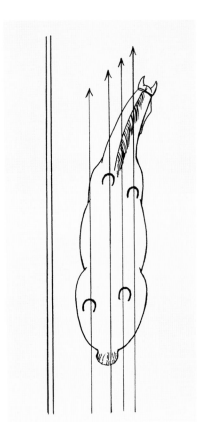

little round your inside leg, flexed to the inside, of course, and moving on up the track. Here's how to do it.

- Have your horse in a good walk and normal contact.

- Walk on the track (say right rein) towards a corner of the school.

- On reaching the corner, put your inside (right) seat bone forward and press with your outside rein against the horse's lower neck.

- Look to your right and walk a small circle, looking well round it all the time and with your horse flexed round your inside leg.

- Come back to the track, maintaining the flexion to the right, and pretend that you are going to continue your circle.

- As you come round the corner, let the forehand move one step off the track as if continuing the circle, and then switch seat bones – that is, put your left seat bone forward instead of your right, and weight it.

- Look to your left up the track and squeeze on and off, or tap, with your inside (right) leg just behind the girth – and your horse will magically do shoulder-in up the track. The trick is in the changing round of the seat bones and in putting your weight, and your eyes, where you want to go.

Don't do too many steps at first – two may be enough – then put your right seat bone forward again and look right, and continue off on a normal circle. Alternatively, some people release the inside flexion and let the horse straighten himself up on to the track. Repeat on the other rein, reversing the aids.

The important point is that the horse has flexed slightly round your leg whilst travelling ahead, and so worked his muscles and joints in a way he never can on a straight line or normal circle. Practise this in walk and trot.

Shoulder-out on a straight line (also called counter shoulder-in) serves the same purposes as shoulder-in but is slightly more difficult as the horse does not have the school fence for guidance. The horse is again flexed away from his direction of movement with his shoulders out on the track and his hindquarters into the school a little. There are a few ways of getting into it, but this way is simple:

■ Walk on the right rein down a long side of the school.

■ On reaching the corner, look round to your right and do a half-circle (maximum 10 m) with your horse slightly flexed round your right leg.

Pauline and Rose perform a shoulder-in which is very hard to fault. Pauline is asking for the movement and direction by placing the right side of her body up the track, looking where she wants to go and weighting her outside seat bone a little. Rose is walking calmly in good posture in response. The fact that they are heading for the gate may be helping!

- *Keeping the slight right flexion*, look at the track and walk in a straight line towards it.

- As the horse's head comes over the inside track, keep the right flexion, put your left seat bone forward and some weight down your left leg, and look to your left up the track. (You are now on the left rein, of course.) Keep the shoulders out on to the track by pressing the left rein against the horse's lower neck.

- Tap or squeeze with your right leg just behind the girth to ask the horse to move up the track.

- After two or three steps, release the right flexion, bring your left seat bone level with your right again and let the horse straighten himself up. Keep looking up to where you want to go.

- Continue on the left rein and repeat the exercise the other way, so you end up on the right rein again.

Practise this in walk and trot.

Shoulder-in on a circle supples and works the horse more but the horse first needs to be familiar with and proficient at shoulder-in on straight lines. Riders often become confused with this exercise as the aids are slightly different. Try it this way:

- On a 20 m circle to the right, walk your horse actively, both of you in good posture, with a comfortable, 'hand-holding' contact on your outside rein (in this case, the left) and a lighter inside rein asking for slight right flexion.

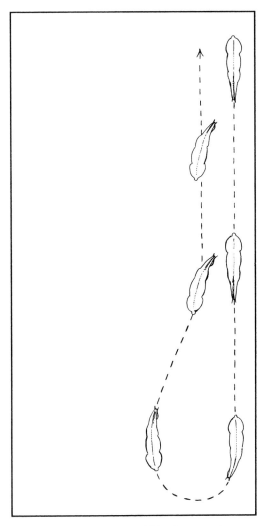

This diagram shows a simple way of getting into the shoulder-out exercise.

- Prepare the movement by looking around your circle and picturing to your horse what you are both going to do. Breathe calmly and rhythmically with him (if you can possibly sense this), or in time with his footfalls if you can't – probably one breath in for four footfalls and one breath out for the next four, and so on.

- Move your right, inside seat bone forwards slightly, weighting it and your right leg a little to encourage the horse to move in off the circle a little.

- Support this aid by pressing sideways with your outside, left, rein on his neck just in front of the withers to bring his forehand just to the inside of the circle.

- Push the horse, with intermittent squeezes of your inside (right) leg, along the circle in this slightly diagonal angle, your outside (left) leg back from the hip to keep his hind feet on the circle track.

- After a very few comfortable steps, release the shoulder-in aids and resume riding your circle.

- Repeat on the other rein.

For *shoulder-out on a circle*, let's say to the left, prepare as in the first three points above for shoulder-in, on a left circle.

- Change the flexion to a slight right one and put your right seat bone forward a little, slightly weighting it and your right leg to encourage the horse to move out off the circular track a little.

- Support this aid by pressing with your left rein sideways on his neck just in front of the withers to bring his forehand just to the outside of the circle.

- Push the horse, with intermittent squeezes of your right leg, along the circle in this slightly diagonal angle, your left leg back from the hip to keep his hind feet on the track of the circle.

- Again, after a very few comfortable steps, release the shoulder-out positioning aids and resume riding on your left circle with a slight left flexion.

If you feel you cannot do the shoulder-in and -out on a circle without a teacher present to show you how to go on at first, that is fine. These suppling and strengthening exercises, which also develop your horse's concentration and ability to think, can be an aim for the near future.

It is most important that you remain calm and relaxed when you do all these exercises, as your horse will definitely take his cue from you and become tense if you are. A tense horse cannot work effectively so you are not only wasting your time but also possibly being counter-productive, giving your horse an unhappy impression which will not bode well for your future relationship.

Work on slopes

Working up and down slopes in the ground improves the horse's balance and encourages him to bring his hindquarters under him. Find undulations in the land on showgrounds and other venues and use them to your benefit. Also, check if any manège you are using has even a slight slope to it and use that, too.

Working up slopes generates thrust from the hindquarters and encourages the horse to come into a good posture as he must lower his head even a little, depending on the slope. Working down slopes brings the hindquarters underneath and you will need a light seat so as not to burden them unnecessarily.

Poles and jumping

Pole work (see Chapter 6), helps to correct posture and, therefore, muscle use if done correctly, making the horse lower his head a little, lift his legs and work carefully and athletically.

Jumping for gymnastic purposes is enjoyed by many horses whether or not their actual job involves leaving the ground. The obstacles should be small but varied, including anything suitable that presents itself out hacking, such as fallen tree trunks or small ditches. Use your imagination to create different combinations of pole patterns and jumps, all aimed at both enjoyment and developing strength and athleticism. Small obstacles can be tackled several days a week but, as they get bigger during your horse's progress, jumping days should get fewer.

Gymnastic jumping is enjoyable and gives horse and rider variety, and also develops muscles, strength and agility – which are always beneficial. This pair are jumping in nice style and the horse has good freedom of the head and neck, with the rider in balance and folded down, not in front of the movement.

Grid work is used by many trainers but you have to build it up gradually or the horse will lose his posture towards the end of a line, might go too fast and struggle, or get tired and make a mess of it, none of which does his attitude or confidence any good and it does not help him physically. Start by putting a small cross-pole at the end of a line of six ground-poles, then remove, say, the third pole and put a very low single cross-pole, maybe with a ground line pole under it, and progress like that so that the horse gets used to meeting different types of obstacles, becoming agile and thinking quickly. The ultimate is a grid of six small jumps set at his normal canter stride with one non-jumping stride between each. As always, don't overdo it.

Correct rest and relaxation

When you have worked your horse in the exercises described in walk and hopefully in trot, he will have worked quite hard and will need to walk around on a free rein to relax for several minutes. Sit lightly with quiet seat and legs and do not give him any more directions than necessary, so that he can partly switch off and relax.

If he lowers his head and neck and voluntarily stretches them right down, you will know that he has worked correctly and is relieving his muscles. If you teach him the command 'head down' you can encourage him to do this: some horses who have never been allowed to stretch properly under saddle are reluctant to do so, so be aware of this and actively encourage your horse in this if he doesn't offer it.

To teach 'head down', start from the ground and take advantage of most horses' inclination to copy you and adapt to you. Stand by his head, bend down and point to the floor, saying his name. If, or more likely when, he drops his head to see what is there, say 'head down' so that he associates the command with the movement. Have a titbit on the floor, or ready in your hand, to give him *whilst his head is down* as a pleasant, positive association with this movement. If he does not lower his head to your point, let him smell the titbit, drawing it down and only giving it to him when his muzzle is almost on the floor. As he is dropping his head, say 'head down' and immediately give him his treat. Do not tease him with it and make him wait; this is unfair, domineering and will not pleasantly reinforce his correct response.

It is imperative for the health and development of muscles that, throughout schooling and working, the horse is not kept in hand (in an 'outline', 'on the bit' or 'in the frame') for more than a very few minutes. The muscles need to relax and the body needs to be free to move and stretch so that the blood can flow freely through the muscles and service them at frequent periods during gymnastic and demanding work. If the horse is not given frequent rest and stretch periods every few minutes (five or so, depending on his development) this cannot happen, tissue health will be compromised and the horse will be on his way to becoming 'muscle bound', stiff and cumbersome.

This condition can be seen in many horses ridden in 'an outline' most of the time without adequate rest and stretch periods, and also in human athletes who do not understand the principles behind muscle health. Most serious, modern athletes have access to qualified, knowledgeable trainers, either personal or club and team trainers, and serious equestrian competitors, mainly at the higher levels, understand the need for alternating work with frequent rest and stretch periods. At the lower amateur levels, however, I find that these principles are often not even thought of, to the detriment of the horses involved.

This voluntary stretching on the part of your horse should be done between exercises, too, so that the blood can flow freely through the muscles to service them as mentioned above. This not only brings oxygen and nutrients to refuel them but removes the toxins which will have formed, thereby relieving any feeling of muscle fatigue and maintaining a healthy biochemical environment within the tissues, which will enable the horse to work again in comfort and, we hope, with enthusiasm.

Standing still and resting on a free rein for a few minutes is also beneficial for a horse. For this, the rider needs to hold the reins at the buckle (and it is surprising how many are reluctant to do this), and the reins need to be long enough to

Vicky is letting Sky stretch right down after a very few minutes work. This allows him to relax physically and mentally, rests the muscles and allows blood to flow freely through them, maintaining their health.

let the horse stretch his muzzle to the ground without the rider having to lean forward or put the hands forward. If you do not hold the reins at the buckle but simply give the horse a *long* rein instead of a *free* one, he will sense the restriction and will not stretch. Of course, if he *asks* to stretch you must release the reins at once and let him, otherwise he will receive the message that he is not allowed or able to do so.

Raising the pulse

If your planned work is going to involve any active or strenuous work at faster gaits, you now need to raise the horse's pulse more by faster and stronger canter work in a good posture. This raises his temperature, too, and ensures that the deeper muscle tissues are warmed up and freely supplied with blood and lymph in readiness for the work to come.

If you only have access to a manège, this work may be slightly limited – although any venue at which you are going to perform active work such as cross-country should offer suitable and more spacious working-in facilities.

It's time to raise the pulse and this is the way to do it, with a good hand-gallop or three-quarter speed canter. Horse and rider are swinging along in good style, the horse is able to breathe freely and move his head and neck fairly freely but the rider keeps control with a neat, balanced position. Her happy attitude will rub off on her horse, who looks quite content.

Try to give your horse a controlled short spin in canter or a three-quarter speed hand-gallop to get things really moving in his body, and try to repeat it up a slight incline. Ask him to work equally on both canter leads and do not let him go flat in the back, put his head up and pull you both along, as this will do his muscles and joints, his way of going and also his mind no good at all. A fairly-treated, reasonably well-schooled and disciplined horse should not be too difficult to keep in hand. Maintain the attitude that, although enjoyable, this is part of his work. Decide for yourself whether this type of working-in is best performed alone or with another horse, either for encouragement or the maintenance of a calm attitude.

The value of this work, with its faster speed, longer strides and more stretched-out body is that it not only warms up the deeper tissues and increases blood flow through them but also puts the joints through a wider range of movement, which is necessary to establish optimum flexibility. The downside of it is that your horse may take hold and cart you into the next county. If you are concerned about this, you need to talk to your teacher about schooling techniques which will give you greater control. It is not beneficial for the horse to be pulling hard at you because, again, this promotes the wrong muscle development, is bad for his mouth and gives him the impression that he can do what he wants under saddle. Horses form habits very easily and you want them to be the right ones.

More stretching

After this fairly taxing workout, a horse is fully prepared for the work to come with one exception. He needs to be stretched to iron out any little knots in his muscles and to increase the 'extensibility' of his tissues. This is not only good for muscle health and function but has long-term beneficial effects on the horse's flexibility, action, performance, agility, strength and suppleness.

The same suppling or loosening exercises you did before mounting can be used for stretching, but they are done in a slightly different way. Now, you have to actually stretch the tissues carefully, as I will explain shortly. This is another topic to cover with a trained equine bodyworker in a formal lesson, if you so wish, but any sensible – and sensitive – owner can do these stretches carefully and beneficially.

Try to go to some high-level competitions such as (particularly) three-day events and note the routines the horses' carers and riders put their horses through. Try to follow one or two horses through cross-country day and make written notes of what happens, as far as you can get access to them. You will note what a lot of trouble the connections take with these equine athletes to warm up and work in before competing and to cool down and warm down afterwards. They do not go to the trouble of doing all this for nothing or because they are unduly fussy. People working at this level are taking advantage of the relatively new discipline of equine sports science and they understand how important correct body-care is to working horses; how it can improve their health, how it can extend their working lives and how it can make them more comfortable and, therefore, resistance-free and capable in their work. All competition horses deserve this care, whatever their discipline, including eventers, dressage and showing horses and ponies, endurance horses, gymkhana ponies, show jumpers, driving horses, Western horses, polo ponies and racehorses. Sadly, many of them are not given the benefits of it.

This does not apply only to high-level competitors, but to any horse working to his own personal best, whether in competition or not. Active hacking, organized rides, park and farm rides, cross-country work, schooling and lessons, hunting and any demanding activity takes its toll on a horse. So does age, and carefully done massage and stretching greatly benefit older horses who are naturally becoming stiffer with the passage of time.

As a trained shiatsu therapist, I understand very well how beneficial shiatsu is as both a therapy and a health maintenance modality for humans and animals in all categories, with its emphasis on energy flow and meridian work and also manipulations, rotations, suppling exercises and stretches.

You may not understand exactly what the carers and therapists working with those horses you are observing are doing, but note down what they do and the order in which they do it, then book an appointment with an expert such as a sports massage therapist or physiotherapist later to discuss it all. The books listed in the Further Reading section at the end of this book will help you greatly and you will also find sources for learning more about these things in the Useful Contacts section.

After demanding work, the natural tendency of muscles is to stay in slight tension or contraction as a defensive measure against further movement. This is also a natural reaction to injury to prevent further stress and, as a result, pain. During work, little injuries, strains and tears can easily occur, unnoticed by us. If these are not treated or removed by stretching and massage, they can easily, over time, result in shortening and restricting a horse's action and making him stiff – perhaps suffering low-grade pain – so he will be less able to work as well as he otherwise could. He may continue to perform *quite* well, his gradually decreasing abilities being put down to increasing age, individual constitution and having worked hard. However, with a regular and correct massage, and a suppling and stretching regime, his working life, abilities and enthusiasm can all be extended and enhanced.

Many older horses are able to stay in reduced work with the help of nonsteroidal anti-inflammatory drugs (NSAIDs) such as phenylbutazone or suxibuzone. They may have osteoarthritis, but stiffened and shortened tissues can also be part of the picture. Appropriate body-care, including regular and correct stretching, can greatly reduce these problems.

There are some essential points to observe about stretching:

- Stretches must not be performed on tissues that are cold and not warmed up, as this can cause injury. They can be applied after massage, after a warm-up, after working in and after cooling and warming down.

- They must not be performed on areas of already injured tissue.

- They must not be performed on older horses with existing problems such as osteoarthritis, chronic tissue damage or marked stiffness without first seeking expert advice, initially from your veterinary surgeon, who can then refer your horse to a physiotherapist and/or sports massage therapist – although you may have to request this.

The benefits of stretching are:

- It helps prevent future injuries.

- It produces long-term lengthening of tissues.

- It improves the scope, flexibility and quality of the horse's action.

- It reduces the aches and pains inherent in a working life.

- It improves the horse's agility, nervous transmission and muscle function.

- It makes the whole body more resilient and resistant to concussion, stress and strain.

- It clearly makes the horse feel good, which can only help his attitude to his life and work – and to you because you are a big part of them.

Review the suppling exercises detailed in Chapter 5 for carrying out before work. The ones you can use for a 'beginner's' stretching programme are the leg stretches forwards and backwards as these affect most of the horse's muscles in his fore-hand, back, loins and hindquarters. The active neck stretches can also be done by offering the horse titbits to encourage him to stretch himself.

Essential points to always have in mind are:

1. Stand as described, with a stable base of support and hold and support the limbs as recommended. Keep your back straight and flat, bending from your hip joints, not your waist. For lifts, use your knees, thigh and seat muscles, not your back, and when supporting the horse's weight place an elbow on your knee so that the weight is transferred to it, relieving your back and arms.

2. Don't forget to breathe as you work! Breathe out as you make an effort and breathe normally and in a relaxed way when holding a stretch.

3. Always work on a non-slip surface and make sure the horse is standing evenly and is well balanced before lifting any leg.

4. Try to have someone sensible holding your horse at his head rather than tying him up, just in case he objects.

5. If he does object, don't force the issue but reassure him and try again, tactfully.

6. Remember that horses unused to bodywork may be a little concerned and may take a few sessions to get used to it.

To do an actual stretch, lift the leg and take it to your intended position, as in the suppling version of the exercise described earlier. Without in any way trying to force matters, hold the leg at the end of its range of movement without pulling or actually trying to stretch it for, ideally if the horse will permit it, ten seconds. If he is used to the suppling exercises, the horse will probably permit this length of hold if you are gentle but firm and supportive, with a positive attitude. Talk to your horse to reassure him in this slightly different procedure.

When you feel him relax his muscles and 'give' you his leg at the apparent end of its range, extend it a *fraction* more to exert a slight stretch on his tissues and try to hold it for ten to twenty seconds. Then slowly release it and put the leg down yourself, praising the horse.

If the horse holds back, just talk to him and tactfully resist but *do not pull the leg*. If he insists and takes the leg away from you, let go. Stroke him and try again. This time he will be more co-operative.

Do not worry if you cannot perform the stretches first time. The horse may never have experienced anything like this and needs time to get used to it. Stay calm and positive and try to do modified stretches, or just hold as in the suppling version of the exercises, but for a little longer. Treat each leg and then praise him. He will become proficient in helping you to help him with time.

Note: If you are not happy about doing stretches on your horse without some prior tuition and demonstration, and cannot arrange for someone else whom you trust to do them, don't worry. You can achieve similar results by leading, lungeing or long-reining your horse in a swinging-on walk with a completely free, low head and neck, over poles, in circles down to 5 m, if only in walk, moving his forehand and hind quarters sideways to both sides to stretch the outside tissues, and generally encouraging full and forward movement. This will all relax the horse mentally and, because he will be using his muscles in an unrestricted, natural way, it will ensure an efficient supply of blood, lymph and energy. These two factors will help to 'pull' out any small clamped-up areas in his muscles, relieve general tension after fairly hard work, stretch muscles, tendons and ligaments naturally and increase their range of movement (and, therefore, your horse's length of stride and action), make him feel much better and thus keep him happier in his work.

After his warm-up and work-in, whether it has been a full or a shortened version, let your horse relax for some time and watch him. If he is fit for the work to come, he will not appear tired. Check his pulse after his vigorous work-in session and when it is back to warm-up level at about 60–80 bpm he could start moderate work. However, many people like to see it back to a resting rate of roughly 35–42 bpm to make sure that the horse is rested but still primed for work, as it were. In a fit horse this will be well within an hour.

You may well be thinking that the warming-up and working-in regime described is far too time-consuming and unnecessary and there is no way you will ever do it. What has been described above is giving you all the options to study: towards the end of this book, routines will be given for days when you have plenty of time and the horse is going to be doing demanding work, either fast work or gymnastically taxing work; for days when you have not so much time and the horse is doing more moderate work; and for days when you are fairly rushed but need to work or exercise your horse.

SUMMARY – WORKING IN

- The four things you need to know are:
  1. How to recognize when a riding horse is going well or badly.
  2. How to feel when a horse you are riding is going well or badly.
  3. How your riding can affect a horse for better or worse.
  4. How to recognize a horse's emotions.

- Try to maintain the 'vertebral bow' posture when working a horse as this is a strong, safe posture in which to carry weight.

- Give the horse very frequent breaks every few minutes, allowing him to stretch his muzzle right down to the ground in order to stretch his muscles and allow them to work naturally. This also permits free blood flow through the tissues, essential to provide nutrients and oxygen and remove the waste products of work.

summary continues ▶

- Do not 'drill' your horse with unnecessary, or unnecessarily forceful, work. This does not help him physically and it is mentally distressing, none of which make for an optimal or co-operative performance.

- Teach your horse to go in self-balance from an early stage. This can then lead to actual self-carriage later on. In self-balance, the horse does not use the bit for support but as a means, and only one means, of receiving messages from his rider. He remains light in hand and, therefore, is much more agile, manoeuvrable and able to move well.

- Do not confuse speed with impulsion. Impulsion means that a horse is moving forward in good balance from the powerful and controlled thrust of his hindquarters. If the horse is simply going fast, 'faster than he can', he is not balanced and cannot possibly avoid going on his forehand.

- Working in involves getting the horse working more gymnastically to prepare him for the active work to come, making him stronger, more agile and more responsive.

- Exercises for working in depend on the level of the horse's schooling and on his fitness and development. They could constitute transitions, lengthening and shortening of stride, large circles and circles spiralling in to the size the horse can do comfortably and then back out again, lateral work, pole work, grid work and gymnastic jumping over small obstacles.

- Faster and more active work raises the horse's pulse to pre-work levels and is needed to prepare him correctly for strenuous work.

- After the work-in is completed, dismounted stretching exercises can be carried out to treat the muscles after this activity and enable them to start the work proper in the best condition. The same exercises as for suppling can be used, but with an element of stretch.

- If you cannot do the stretching exercises, you can achieve similar results by dismounting and lungeing, long-reining or leading your horse with a completely free head and neck over poles, on 5 m circles and in any exercises that involve his crossing both front and hind legs to stretch the tissues on the sides of the limbs and body. This also relaxes the horse and promotes good circulation.

- When your horse's heart rate/pulse is back to around warm-up rate (about 80 bpm), which should be within twenty minutes, he is ready to start your intended work.

CHAPTER 10

Factors affecting planned work

Your horse is finally ready to do his job. This may be a schooling session, a lesson, or an active ride or drive of some sort including hunting or competing at any level.

In a schooling session, the horse is ready after the preparatory work to improve existing movements, learn new exercises or movements, learn different jumping and striding skills and so on, according to his level of schooling and training.

General welfare

A generation ago it was still commonly believed that once a horse or pony began his actual work his welfare became of secondary consideration to performance. This was actually stated in some highly-respected books on horse management – but fortunately things have changed. Horses in countries where equestrianism is a popular sport are no longer essential for warfare or transport and their welfare is not of secondary importance to their jobs.

It is just as important for a horse's well-being to be considered during work as during training. Whether the horse is being schooled or is doing his job using the skills and capabilities he has already, every opportunity should be taken to allow him to rest and revitalize himself.

Certainly he needs to be allowed to stretch his head and neck right down, as described earlier, at very frequent intervals for muscle health and by way of a mental break (no schooling 'in outline' for virtually the whole session, as is often done). If hacking or doing roadwork on quiet roads, certainly do not keep the horse in hand, on the bit or 'in an outline' most of the time. (Although when riding on busy or potentially dangerous roads, it is prudent to have the horse 'in hand' to the extent that he is reasonably attentive and able to respond promptly to any aids necessary for safety.) This is a common mistake and is not good for the horse. Schooling can be done out hacking, of course, but, as in a manège, the horse must be allowed to stretch frequently and learn to walk out, otherwise he will experience muscle pain and distress, and develop a shortened walk. Hacking out with the horse on the bit all the time is a very quick way to ruin both his walk and his willingness and is just as bad as keeping him 'in and up' all the time in a manège.

Horses working in fast gaits and jumping need to get their breath back, those doing work demanding stamina at fast gaits, such as hunters and steeplechasers, need a chance to get their 'second wind' and, depending on a horse's actual job, he needs a chance to stale, and to have a drink and maybe a small feed. Show days may be fun for owners but a wearying trial for their horses, even if they are competing in classes that do not make great physical demands on them. Between classes, they need to relax, have hay, feed, water, grass if available (and it is on most venues where horses gather) and to be allowed to stale. Most horses will not do this until they are compelled to if they are left in a vehicle or tied up anywhere, which is very poor horse care.

Preventing dehydration

When horses work, especially in warm or hot weather, they become hot and so they sweat. Sweating is one way for a horse to lose excess heat and ward off hyperthermia or heat exhaustion. As sweat is excreted it picks up heat from blood circulating in the capillaries in the skin layers (sweat and blood both being liquid and, therefore, good conductors of heat). The sweat reaches the outer layer of skin and evaporates into the drier air, taking the heat with it.

When sweat is lost, the whole body, including the blood, loses water and the blood becomes 'thicker'. This makes it more difficult for it to be pumped round the body, which can strain the heart. The blood having lost some of its water and, therefore, its volume, the horse cannot sweat so much and so he fails to cool off. The blood obviously cannot do its main job so well – that of carrying oxygen and nutrients and removing waste products. The horse becomes short of oxygen and the body starts working anaerobically (without oxygen), which results in lactic acid forming. This makes the horse feel very fatigued, causes muscle pain and damage, and even collapse. The horse may develop rhabdomyolysis (azoturia or tying up) because of muscle injury from the lactic acid, and show colic symptoms. As the condition progresses, the horse, being unable to lose heat efficiently through sweating, starts breathing very quickly, even panting like a dog, to try to lose heat from the lungs that way.

If the horse's rate of respiration ever approaches or exceeds the pulse rate, call a vet without delay.

When offering water to a horse who is (or may become) hot, it is a good plan to offer the horse a drink of plain water and one with electrolytes in it so that he can take which he prefers. The electrolytes will help to ward off dehydration, which can be more of a problem than many people realize. Horses who don't like drinking unfamiliar-tasting water may be happy to drink water in which sugar beet pulp has been soaked (this also provides electrolytes and some energy). Be careful in warm weather that it has not gone 'off'; probably one of the quick-soak types would be safer. Horses may be accustomed to drinking anywhere by always adding a little apple or peppermint essence to their water at home and away. Taking water from home in large containers is always a good idea, so that it can at least be mixed with any local water available. Horses' drinking habits away from home often change and you may need to try placing an individual's (familiar) bucket in different places and at different heights in a strange stable. Very many horses will not drink stale or tepid water, but will drink freely if the water is fresh and cold. Drinking can be a dangerous procedure for feral horses and this instinct may pass down to domestic horses, many of whom do not drink away from home until they have settled and feel secure. This can be a significant problem because of the threat of dehydration, so take it seriously and don't just assume that your horse is not thirsty. Occasionally, you may have to syringe some water into his mouth to get him to start drinking.

The most reliable test for dehydration is the capillary refill test, which can detect even slight dehydration: press the horse's gum above one of his upper corner teeth with your thumb to create a pale patch. It should become pink again within 1½ seconds. Another common test, the skin pinch test, will show up significant dehydration: pinch up a fold of skin at the bottom of the horse's neck just in front of his shoulder. If he is *not* dehydrated it should fall back flat immediately, but if it stays up in a fold for even a second, he is.

Maintaining energy levels

Small feeds given when possible help the horse to refuel fairly quickly during a long drawn-out competition or on a long day, and for this purpose they must be easily digested. They could comprise cereals that have been extruded or micronized (forms of cooking to make them easy to eat and digest) plus soaked sugar beet pulp. This will have a little sugar left in it after most has been extracted for the human food market, but its energy also comes from its fibrous structure. Molasses and sugar are misunderstood elements in a horse's diet, and the addition of molasses to feeds (maybe in some very sloppy sugar beet pulp) boosts the energy content, too. A little high-energy, short-chopped forage, such as alfalfa can be added. If the breaks in his work are longer, the horse should have hay or haylage to keep him comfortable inside and to avoid disrupting his digestion and possibly suffering colic later on. The hay or haylage should be removed an hour or so before any work that is at all strenuous.

Comfort

During breaks in work, the horse should be protected from extremes of weather. If he is waiting around in the cold, he should have a rug or coat thrown over his back, or at least over his loins and quarters, and be stood in as sheltered a spot as possible.

In hot, sunny weather, find some shade for him and stand him with his head facing into a breeze, if possible. It is very bad practice to stand horses inside hot, stuffy vehicles or stables in hot weather and this can bring on hyperthermia, which can kill horses if not relieved. Even susceptible horses turned out without adequate shade in hot, sunny weather can suffer from this and become ill or even die. The signs of hyperthermia are very like those of dehydration – lethargy, disorientation and lack of co-ordination, plus lack of desire to eat or drink. Also, use a good fly repellent on your horse. Being pestered can prevent him relaxing, and make him stressed and irritable.

If appropriate, it is refreshing for the horse to have his tack removed during breaks in his work; he will rest and relax better if there is no bit in his mouth and no girth round his ribcage. Sponging him down will cool and refresh him in hot weather, and grazing in hand for a while calms his mind and stretches his body, because his head and neck are down. It also helps him to refuel because of the natural energy in the grass.

If the horse is wearing studs in his shoes, do not let him stand around on hard ground with them in. This will force him to stand unevenly and use his muscles to balance and try to get comfortable. It also stresses the feet (which will be unbalanced), his limbs all the way up to his shoulders and hips, and his back. When he is standing naturally without studs this is not a problem and, of course, horses can doze and sleep lightly standing up, but when wearing studs on hard ground none of this is possible. If you have no other choice, remove them.

SUMMARY – FACTORS AFFECTING PLANNED WORK

- Keep your horse's welfare uppermost in your mind during work. If at any time you sense that he is not coping, stop the work or withdraw from the competition.

- Do not keep your horse 'in an outline' for more than a very few minutes at a time and then only if he is capable of holding this himself. If out hacking or doing anything similar, do not ride him in this way all the time, which is often seen and is a very common and damaging mistake.

- During work which is sustained, maybe over a few hours such as several classes at a show or competition, an endurance ride (or even at shorter distances) or a day ride, give your horse every opportunity to rest and relax, stretch fully, stale, have a short graze or small feed and a drink when convenient and, as far as possible, do not expose him to extremes of weather.

- At any time of year – but particularly in hot, humid or sunny weather – keep a close eye on your horse for signs of overheating and/or dehydration, keep him as cool as you can and let him drink more or less when he wants to.

- In cold, wet, windy weather, protect your horse as much as you reasonably can. Don't let him stand out in such weather when he is hot: find some shelter and/or keep him walking with a rug over him.

- If your horse's respiration ever approaches or exceeds his pulse rate, call a vet immediately. Do not wait for the horse to recover on his own or 'see how he goes on'.

- When possible, remember that it is refreshing for the horse to have all his tack removed and to be sponged down.

- Do not let him stand around on hard footing with studs in his shoes, as these unbalance his feet, affect his stance and involve unaccustomed muscle use, which is a strain to him.

PART **3**

Aftercare

CHAPTER 11

Cooling down

A short walk home

Once your horse's actual work has finished, you or your helpers still have quite a lot to do.

The old advice to always 'walk the first mile out and the last mile home' is as relevant now as it was then. The horse has warmed up and worked in, he has done his work, and he must now be cooled down and, to use the modern term, 'warmed down' gradually.

If you have been out for a long or active hack, either just for fun or as part of a horse's fitness programme, it is a good idea, when a couple of miles from home, to walk him on a free rein, commensurate with control and conditions in the surrounding area. Let him stretch out and along with his head and neck swinging. Don't flop about in the saddle, as this makes it harder work for him to carry you; sit erect and still with a quiet seat and legs and keep your hands down and still on the buckle end of the reins.

In a quiet area with good all-round visibility that allows you to watch for traffic, it is a good plan to let the horse walk in the middle of the road so that he is not bracing himself against the camber all the time. Much depends on the roads and the availability of tracks in your area, but when you can do so, it is better to avoid making your horse walk on a sideways slope such as the camber of a surfaced highway. Many people do not understand this aspect of hacking out and wonder why young or green (or sensible!) horses always wander into the middle of the road or on to the pavement: it is because they find walking on the camber so uncomfortable. In fact, it can actually result in uneven muscle development and stressed legs because of the uneven forces passing up the legs. A friend of mine, who was a farrier, used to walk his horses on the opposite side of the road whenever it was safe to do so, to even them up.

When you are about a mile from home, consider dismounting and walking the rest of the way home. This will relax and relieve your horse even more, and will certainly help you to loosen up, too. Loosen your girth a hole before you dismount so that it does not suddenly feel tighter to the horse when your weight, which has been pressing it down, comes off the saddle. Then run up your stirrups, loosen your girth another hole or two (leaving it just tight enough to keep the saddle safely in place) and maybe loosen your noseband, too – although it should not be so tight that the horse needs to be relieved of it. Bring the reins over your horse's head (unless he is wearing a martingale) and use them together like a lead rope, holding them properly for safety. Remember that, whenever you are leading a horse on a road, you must be on the same side and going in the same direction as other traffic, and walk between your horse and the traffic, partly to control your horse (if you have a whip, carry it in your outside hand) and partly because, whilst some motorists will think nothing of 'buzzing' a horse they will think twice about buzzing you (and if they do, try to get their registration number and report them for dangerous driving).

If the horse has been schooling or having a lesson, a good way to finish off after the end of the session is, again, to walk around for several minutes on a free rein. If your horse is rather warm and sweating, trot him around on a long rein for ten minutes or so, ridden or led, to keep the blood circulating, bringing oxygen and nutrients to the muscles and removing waste products. Then come down to an active, free walk. Let him have a few short drinks in between walking around, but keep him moving until he is cooler and is breathing more normally. If the weather is cold, put a rug on him during this process.

(It may seem that if the horse is blowing and tired it is not appropriate to make him trot and walk around and that rest is what he needs. Apart from the important fact already mentioned about his muscles needing to have a good blood flow through them to restore and 'cleanse' them, it is known that, whilst a horse is moving, air continues to flow more freely over his body to cool him, and also when the heart (and, therefore, the blood flow) slows down, the horse's temperature can actually rise, sometimes to dangerous levels. Blood carries heat, which is radiated out through the skin, so we should try to keep things moving gently to assist all these processes.)

If the horse has been working harder, perhaps at a competition, and is hot and tired, with his temperature, pulse and respiration rates all up, this cooling down period should be longer. If the weather is cold, keep him covered as you trot and walk him round and ideally try to find somewhere under cover (or at least as sheltered as you can) to do this part of the process. Try not to skimp on this, as it is important. If it is hot you may need some cool or cold water to use as described below, and to find a shady spot with a good airflow to walk him and rinse him off.

Your aim should be to get all his rates back down to warm-up rates within twenty minutes and to resting rates within an hour: if this does not happen, consult a vet.

I feel that it is more comfortable for the horse to have his saddle and bridle removed pretty soon rather than leaving them on. Horses always enjoy having their bits removed and they relax more quickly and readily when they are untacked and led around and cooled down with just a comfortable headcollar on (and maybe a rug or sheet, depending on conditions). Some people, though, do believe that the saddle should stay on to prevent the capillaries in the back refilling too quickly and rupturing. I have never done this and have never had any problems. The capillaries are hair-fine and react quickly, so the very act of your loosening the girth and dismounting will remove pressure from them. I have mentioned it to a couple of vets with no conclusion either way, so the decision is yours.

If you are between classes, sections or phases of a competition, you may not be able to remove the tack, of course, but it should be loosened and the horse refreshed by sponging down (especially his head, face and hindquarters), having a drink and so on. This is also a good opportunity to give the horse a fresh girth and numnah, sponging down the saddle and girth areas to cool and freshen him up, and maybe changing the bit, if appropriate. A change can be refreshing, and as good as a rest. If there is time before starting work again, he can have a small, easily-digested feed, as described earlier.

How to cool down a horse

First of all, if he is clearly hot, sweating and blowing you need to know what his temperature is, so take it as described in Chapter 2. It should never rise more than 2 °C (or about 4 °F) above his normal at-rest rate. If it is this high or very nearly so, contact a vet. Also check whether or not he is dehydrated.

In cool to cold weather

In these conditions you will just need a suitable rug to cover your horse as you trot and then walk him around. Every few minutes, give him a drink of aired water (water with just the chill taken off it – take a flask of very hot water with you to add to the cold) unless he prefers it cold, and offer an electrolyte drink as well so

he can choose, and let him have about six swallows every ten minutes until his thirst is quenched, after which he can have water available ad lib.

Keep the horse walking around, wearing a medium to lightweight rug; ideally a permeable or loose-weave one that allows the heat out gradually, possibly left open at the chest, and let him cool down that way.

During the cooling down process, walk for a few minutes, then give your horse a short drink, then walk again and so on, until he has had his fill.

In warm to hot weather

In these conditions, find as cool, shady and breezy a spot as you can to do what is known as the 'walk and wash' technique. The muscles hold a lot of blood and cooling it down will cool the muscle tissue very effectively as the cooler blood circulates all around. The body core temperature is also cooled by this technique, which was developed as a result of scientific research relating to international-level competition horses. The old advice of not putting water on the horse's hindquarters because it could cause him to tie up has been found to be inaccurate. These, in fact, are just the areas which need cooling down and the latest research should be followed.

165

Professionals at work. The horse is in the shade and being cooled down with water.

However, in your enthusiasm to cool down your horse, do not suddenly slosh cold water on his hot body, as it will shock him. Start gradually with a damp sponge on his legs and work up his body, using more water. Many people still prefer to use just cool water rather than cold: it will still cool the horse down and encourage evaporation, and is less unpleasant for the horse. *Great care should be taken when using very cold or iced water.* These can rapidly cool down the horse externally, but could also reduce the superficial circulation, keeping heat in the body so that the body core temperature may remain high, causing an actual *delay* in cooling down properly. Take up to date advice from a vet on this matter.

Walk your horse for thirty seconds, then, except in cold weather, wash him down all over with big sponges saturated with water for another thirty seconds. Then walk for another thirty seconds and wash for thirty seconds and so on. If you have helpers, someone can waft the horse with rugs or whatever else suitable is available.

Do not scrape off the water as the wetter he is, the more heat can evaporate from his body. The reason why sweating cools a horse is that it brings heat out of the skin with it. As the moisture/sweat evaporates the heat goes with it, and the same principle applies to water which, being a good conductor of heat, will take up heat from the horse's skin.

Checks in all weathers

In any weather, after five minutes of walking around, take the horse's temperature, then do so again at ten minutes, by which time it should have dropped by 1 ºC or 2 ºF. Continue this cooling regime until his temperature is only 1 ºC or 2 ºF above his normal at-rest temperature, or less.

Watch your horse's demeanour, as well. Feel the skin on his flanks and quarters to check that it is not noticeably cool; check his pulse and respiration rates as well as his temperature and make sure that he is not actually cooled down *too much*.

If he shows any of the following symptoms, call a vet immediately. Do not wait to see how he goes on.

- He looks tucked up, tense and chilly, even shivering.

- He seems lethargic.

- He looks distressed.

- He shows erratic respiration, either very fast or very slow.

- He seems to lack co-ordination and is unsteady.

- He seems not fully aware of his surroundings.

- He has 'thumps'. (The horse will look as though his heart is beating in his flanks and he actually has hiccups caused by stress, overwork and exhaustion.)

Whilst waiting for the vet, put an appropriate rug or sheet on the horse and try to keep him quiet. Lots of people milling around and giving different instructions can oppress and worry the horse – and the owner!

Watch him very closely anyway, even if he does not show any obvious signs of anything amiss and do not hesitate to contact a vet if you have the slightest suspicion that he is not 'right'. If he is not fit to continue with the work ahead – competition or otherwise – withdraw, even if you are part of a team. Your horse's welfare always comes first.

If your horse has to travel home, he should be cooled down, dried, rested and relaxed before the journey, and should also have had what he needs to eat and drink before setting off, plus hay or haylage for the journey.

SUMMARY – **COOLING DOWN**

- Remember 'walk the last mile home' when out on a ride. On a competition or showground, keep the horse trotting, then jogging and finally walking for around ten minutes to keep the blood flowing and removing waste products from his tissues. This keeps the tissues in good health and helps to prevent stiffness and aching muscles next day.

- Keep him walking around for several more minutes, maybe with a rug or sheet over him if chilly or, if it is warm or hot, using the 'wash and walk' technique.

- Let him have short drinks every ten minutes until his thirst is quenched. It is best to offer two types of drinks – one with electrolytes in it, or fresh sugar beet water, and one plain water.

- Within ten minutes, your horse's temperature should have reduced by 1 °Celsius or 2 °F. Within twenty minutes all his rates should be back to warm-up rate. In any weather, continue the cooling regime (walking and washing in hot weather, or leading in hand with a permeable rug on him in cold weather) until his temperature is only 1 °C or 2 °F above his normal at-rest rates.

- If your horse shows any of the symptoms of distress listed above, call a vet. Do not hesitate to withdraw from whatever the work is in this case and do not be persuaded by anyone to continue.

- Before travelling home, the horse should have had an hour's rest, have eaten and drunk and be back to his normal TPR rates.

CHAPTER 12

Warming down

The warming down process after athletic work comes after the actual cooling down, when the horse's TPR rates are back to resting rates, or very nearly so. It is regarded as most beneficial to perform post-work stretches (or alternative groundwork as described earlier) and massage between one and three hours of stopping work. Up to about three hours after work, the tissues are usually still fairly warm and pliable and the most benefit is obtained by treating the horse during this time window. The break before starting this process gives time for checking the horse over, cooling down, resting and refuelling with a small feed and drink and making him comfortable.

If you are travelling home, you will have to decide, therefore, whether or not to do this before you set off. The journey itself will involve muscle use and some stress and the horse will need at least walking around in hand with low head and neck to loosen up after his trip. Whatever your situation, try to make time within the one to three hour period to do at least a basic massage or stroking, and the stretching. It will only take about half an hour, it will benefit your horse greatly and is more important than many owners realize.

Massage and stretching

The type of massage described for the warm-up is ideal to use again now, after work. The effleurage technique is quite simple and calming to the horse; it manipulates and loosens the muscles after work, and stimulates blood flow, all of which aid muscle health.

If you wish, you can simply give your horse a sensitive all-over stroking, but not so light that you have no effect on the muscles. Partly lean your weight, through your flat hands, on to his muscular areas to compress and release them a little, and stroke his legs up towards his body, finishing with a downward sweep to smooth the hair.

Either a basic massage or a stroking technique is easy for an owner to do and feels very therapeutic to a tired and possibly stressed horse. It helps him to feel really good, detects sore areas, assists blood and energy flow to eliminate toxins, 'unties' muscle knots and generally give the horse pleasure as well as benefit.

The stretches are just as described in Chapter 9 for use after the warm-up (as opposed to simply pre-work suppling exercises) – the same movements but with the stretch element. Alternatively, you can work in hand in a structured way aimed at stretching out and 'treating' the muscles to minimize any after-effects of work and help prevent long-term problems such as unrelieved muscle tension (slight contraction), small, tense, hardened areas of cramped-up tissue caused by tiny injuries, shortened action, stiffness and slight pain and an understandably reduced willingness to work.

Grooming for therapy and maintenance

Body-brushing

Giving your horse a proper body-brushing, done in the traditional way, is a form of massage in itself. The time for grooming is after the horse has cooled down and dried off after work, the old reasons being that it is easier to clean a horse when his pores are open and his skin and muscles warm and supple. This is certainly true but correct body-brushing also acts as a massage which both stimulates the skin and relaxes the muscles underneath it because of the pressure on the skin and muscles. The skin is stimulated because of the action of the bristles on it. The whole process also acts as a form of check-up on how he is feeling both inside and out. You notice every little scratch on him, every sore place, find out where he does not like being touched, and you have the opportunity to prove to him that you are not going to hurt him and to train him gradually, maybe by using your hands in 'no-go' areas, to permit all-over handling. This can be crucial when veterinary treatment or first aid is needed, or simply when having to keep the horse decently clean.

This kind of grooming is also great 'bonding time', when your horse knows that you are paying him attention and you can talk to him quietly and fuss him at the same time – but you *must* do it confidently and sensitively, and you need to bear in mind that previous owners may not have done so. Those who do not understand the health and psychological benefits of a confident, sensitive, rhythmic body-brushing often scrub at the horse and irritate, anger or frighten him. They rush the whole process – and horses hate being rushed. Sensitive areas of the horse may receive no consideration and the end result is a horse who hates being groomed and has to be tied up. This makes him feel trapped and forced to accept the almost tortuous process to come, which causes snapping, stamping, kicking and various other defensive and protective behaviours and, all in all, is best not done at all. You might just as well clean him by the modern, widespread methods of just rinsing him down and maybe spraying him with a coat dressing. This will clean the horse and give him a shine, but he will lose out on the benefits of the proper body-brushing. The crazy thing is that the body-brushing takes only a little longer than preparing your equipment, rinsing the horse down and drying him off.

A thorough body-brushing, done in a therapeutic way and without rushing or scrubbing at the horse, acts as a form of massage as well as cleaning the horse and conditioning his skin and coat.

If your horse is very tired after his work, it may be kinder not to groom him but to let him rest, grooming him at the next opportunity after lighter work. You can certainly body-brush your horse at any time, but the best effects are felt and seen after work. The horse can have his hay and chomp away as you work, satisfying his appetite and enjoying his relaxing treatment at the same time. Horses brought up in well-run yards with 'thinking' attendants find great reassurance in this familiar process and settle to it with relaxed enjoyment.

For grooming you will need a traditional body brush with short, fine but stiff, natural bristles. I find that synthetic bristles do not clean the horse so well, can clog with hairs, deform and flatten, and the ends can split and scratch both the coat and the skin. Leather-backed brushes are also easier to use than wooden ones as they are slightly flexible and mould to your hand which, of course, the wooden ones cannot do.

You also need a metal curry comb, either the type with a loop over the back for your hand, or with a wooden handle. This is for cleaning the bristles of your body brush after every couple of strokes or so. It has metal, toothed 'combs' running from side to side across it and you use it by placing the body brush, bristles down, on the curry comb with the teeth running sideways across the bristles. Press the curry comb and the brush together fairly firmly and pull the teeth down the bristles a couple of times. If you then look at the curry comb you will see grease and dandruff in the teeth, which are removed by tapping the comb on a corner on the floor – strictly speaking, by the door, so that the debris can be swept away afterwards.

If it is a nice day, try to groom your horse outdoors or, at least, somewhere other than his own stable, because body-brushing raises the dust and you do not want to contaminate the airspace in which he has to live and breathe. Your horse must be dry and have had any dried mud and sweat cleaned off with the dandy brush or plastic or rubber curries. Start brushing with the body brush backwards and downwards with the lie of the hair. If the horse is very greasy or dirty, you can often use a quick side-to-side stroke with the brush to raise the dirt, then use a normal one to brush it away, ending the stroke by flicking the dirt away from his skin.

It's logical to start at the head, steadying it with one hand and pressing the bristles carefully through the hair to reach the skin. Don't forget to brush under the forelock and jaw and inside the ears. Clean the brush with the curry comb after every few strokes and be very careful not to knock the horse with the brush or comb.

When the head is done, start at the top of the neck and work down it and underneath it, progressing to the shoulders, chest and breastbone between the forelegs, down the forelegs, back to the trunk, under the belly, around the hindquarters, between the hind legs and finally down the hind legs. The areas most often forgotten or skimped are inside the ears, under the forelock, mane and tail, underneath the horse, between the legs and behind the pasterns.

If you are doing the left side, start with the brush in your left hand and the curry comb in your right. Stand a little away from your horse because this will give the extra pressure needed to do this job properly without tiring yourself. The reason for this is that, as with massage, you lean your weight on to the brush rather than pushing it through the coat with your arm and shoulder muscles, which would soon fatigue you. A thorough, full body-brushing takes an experienced groom about half an hour and you won't last this long if you don't use the right technique.

With a slightly stiff arm but with the elbow slightly bent, place the brush on to the coat – do not bang or slap it down – then lean into it and draw it down in the direction of the hair. At the end of the stroke, flick the bristles (and the dirt) up and away from the coat. After two or, at most, three strokes, clean the brush with the curry comb. As the curry comb accumulates the scurf and dirt from the coat, tap it out on its side to clear it. Work systematically all over the horse in this way, keeping up the rhythm where you can, watching closely what you are doing and also your horse's reaction so that you come to know every inch of his skin and coat intimately, noting any lumps and bumps, spots, scratches, wounds, the condition of his coat and so on.

If your arm does get tired, it's fine to change arms rather than continue with an arm too fatigued to do its job. You need, on average, to do about six strokes in one place to clean the coat properly, and a good rhythm is about one stroke a second. This is brisk enough not to dawdle but slow enough to relax your horse. Of course, there are places, such as on the head and legs and underside of the horse, where this long, rhythmic, sweeping motion, leaning your weight into the strokes is not possible – but do it where you can.

If your horse does not like being groomed, use the brush gently at first to accustom him to it, and be prepared to use your hands in particularly difficult areas. Don't force the horse to submit but get him used to it gradually by consistently sensitive handling. But bear in mind that doing things so lightly that you tickle him is as unpleasant as being rough. Always be confident and positive, lightly persistent, but don't push the issue.

When doing the mane and forelock, get right down to the roots to get out the grease, keep cleaning the body brush, and do the mane in locks of hair, working from the poll downwards. To do the tail, separate the hair on the dock and here, too, get right down to the skin. Hold out the tail by the end of the dock and let the hair fall out one lock at a time and brush in a few strokes for each lock from the bottom, working up to the roots. This prevents tightening any tangles and knots in the hair by brushing downwards into them. Many people separate tail hairs just with their fingers, but this is very time-consuming, of course. You must deal with the hair of the mane and tail gently otherwise you will pull out too much or break the strands, and ruin them in no time.

The traditional way to finish off the horse is to bundle up a slightly damp (not wet) cloth called a stable rubber, rather like a tea towel, in your hand and flop it down all over him to remove any dust which may have landed on his coat from the air.

Although this is fairly hard work until you get used to it, the look of your horse's coat will far outshine (literally) that of a horse who is not given the benefit of regular, correct body-brushing. The shine comes from his natural coat oils and lack of dirt and dandruff, and has a deep gloss to it rather than being superficial. The coat also lies closer to the skin, looks sleeker and emphasizes the horse's muscular development in a way that the coats of horses who are over-washed and sprayed can never do. The horse also retains the protection of the natural oils in his skin and coat so his skin will be in much better condition than that of a horse who is frequently bathed with shampoo.

The *limited* use of coat sprays on a clean coat has a place because they help to stop dirt clinging and make the horse easier to groom. This also applies to the mane and tail. Do not, however, apply them to dirty hair as a quick fix instead of grooming, as they do not actually clean the coat.

Wisping

This is another traditional practice which waned in popularity because of the modern curses of time and money constraints, although it never actually died out in the best stables, mainly racing yards. It is returning to popularity because of its undeniable benefits and the fact that it is not difficult to learn to do it properly. It is also known as 'banging' because of how it is done. Some call it 'strapping', although strictly speaking this term is used to describe a combined full grooming (incorporating correct body-brushing) with wisping.

A wisp is a hard pad made from a twisted rope of hay, according to the accompanying drawings and instructions. (You can buy leather or chamois pads for wisping, but in my opinion they are not as good as a proper wisp. They drag and pull on the hair and skin, which is uncomfortable for the horse, and they do not give him that pleasant, stimulating sensation. Also, the chamois ones are not easy to clean.) The wisp is used on areas of muscle-mass only to:

- Loosen out any little areas of muscle cramps or tension.

- Encourage the flow of blood and lymph through the muscles by repeatedly compressing and releasing the tissues.

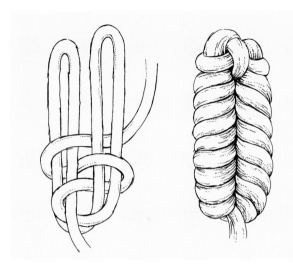

To make a proper wisp, twist a rope of hay or haylage to about your own height, keeping your foot on one end and pulling it taut as you go. Form two loops with the other end and pass the loops alternately around the rest of the rope all the way down to your foot. Tuck the spare end in, as shown, to secure it – and there you have it.

- Develop muscles by causing them to react to the bangs by contracting as the horse anticipates the impact.

- Help squeeze out natural oil (sebum) in the skin and thereby condition it.

The parts of the horse that are wisped are shown on page 176, and are:

- The bottom of the neck below the crest (but steering clear of the vertebrae, gullet and windpipe).

- The muscles behind the shoulder-blades and above the elbows.

- The muscles over the hindquarters and down the backs of the thighs.

Because of the nature of the technique, bony and sensitive areas are not wisped – not only would it do no good; it could do harm. Therefore, the following areas are not done: back, loins, chest, ribcage, forearms and gaskins (second thighs).

The most effective and logical time to wisp is to follow on with it from body-brushing. First dampen the wisp slightly by sprinkling a little water on both sides of it, then stand as for body-brushing, a little away from your horse, with a slightly stiff and bent arm. Lean your weight into the horse and bring the wisp down with a firm but *not hard* slap or 'bang' on the chosen area and, keeping the pressure on, draw it down the hair. Lift up and repeat, spending about twenty minutes to half an hour over the whole process. Turn the wisp when you change sides. As you wisp when your horse is already clean, the wisp should last several sessions before you need to make another one.

The object of using wisping to develop the muscles is to cause them to flinch (contract) in anticipation of the bang. Do about one bang per second, as for

The muscular areas of the horse that are wisped.

Leaning your weight on to your slightly stiffened arm, slap the wisp down on the muscles, firmly but not hard. Draw the wisp down the muscle mass in the direction of the hair. Lift and repeat about six times in one spot.

grooming, and do let your horse eat his hay during the process. The rhythm and the physical sensations that wisping produces are pleasing to most horses but, as with body-brushing, you need to go very lightly, almost just simulating the process, with a horse who hasn't a clue what is happening. When teaching, I always advise clients to stroke their horses, not to pat or, certainly, thump them, as this is similar to the unpleasant feeling of being kicked or bitten when in a herd – a short, sharp, rejecting sensation rather than the smooth pressure of stroking or of horses mutually grooming one another. You would think that horses also regarded wisping as being unfriendly, and those not used to it may well do so, but if you do it following on from grooming and gradually accustom them to it with a stroking technique at first, it is surprising how they not only get used to it but, as with proper body-brushing, come to enjoy it and clearly find it creates a feel-good factor in them.

When, after body-brushing and wisping, you stand back and admire your work, you can feel justly proud of yourself and your horse!

Other techniques

Hand-rubbing can be used to finish off your horse, especially on the areas which are not wisped. Just do it in the same way as the stroking/massaging technique described earlier.

Ear-stripping is another old practice which many horses find very relaxing. You simply stand in front of your horse and encourage him to put his head down; then cup your hands round his ears, fingers pointing away from you, and pull your hands gently up his ears for a minute or so.

Keeping the horse warm

When grooming, massaging, rubbing or wisping, bear in mind the air temperature, especially if your horse is clipped. Keep those parts of him not being worked on covered with his rug, moving it around as necessary. Cold horses, like us, clamp up and cannot get the best benefit from any bodywork treatments. If you are carrying out these treatments outdoors, make sure you are not in a breeze or wind in cold weather – although in summer they might be welcome.

If, in cold weather, your horse is wet for any reason (including washing and sweating) he needs to be protected from the cold, but he needs the air to get to him to help him dry off. Don't forget his neck, which is a significant site for heat loss. Drape another rug over it if he is clipped there.

SUMMARY – **WARMING DOWN**

- Warming down should be carried out between one and three hours after work.

- Use any of the techniques mentioned. Stretches are particularly beneficial and it is very well worth learning to do them properly. Until then, use the alternative in-hand techniques described, such as leading in hand with the head and neck completely free over ground-poles, or on 5 m circles, and ask him to do any movements which involve crossing the legs, all of which stretch the muscles and tissues.

- After stretching, you can massage your horse or give him a relaxing, therapeutic groom and also wisp him. Hand-rubbing can be used instead of massage and many horses find ear-stripping relaxing and comforting.

- Keep your horse comfortably warm with suitable rugs and sheets but do not overload him.

CHAPTER 13

Finishing off

What you do with your horse when you have finished the warm-down depends on how tired he is, also on his normal routine and the time of day.

Freedom

Depending on the weather, he could be turned out to graze, rest, relax and be with his friends – which would be the preferred choice of most horses. Sadly, there is an attitude around today that horses should not be turned out together, or in some cases even at all if they are 'competition horses' (as if they were different from others) in case they damage themselves. Bearing in mind the type of animals horses are – social, grazing, running animals – I think that this is an appalling point of view. I realize that many horses in some of the 'best' establishments of all kinds are not turned out regularly (if at all), but this does not alter the fact that they *should be*. Horses *can* injure themselves in the field, but they can also get injured in the stable, and certainly during the work we make them do. (Often, it is people's very management that make horses ill.) Injury is a risk we have to take if we are going to have horses and be fair to them in exchange for what they do for us.

Another inescapable point is the 'mind damage' caused to horses who are never allowed liberty, or time freely socializing with others of their own kind, not merely over a fence. All this flies in the face of The Five Freedoms which are now being taken more and more as standard guidelines for the care and management of horses and other animals. The fourth 'freedom' is: '*Freedom to express most patterns of normal behaviour by providing sufficient space, proper facilities and company of the animal's own kind.'* This freedom is not addressed by keeping a horse stabled, denying him normal social contact and only allowing him to move when working.

Keeping an athletic, working animal indoors for all but about two hours a day is also not an efficient way of maintaining a fully-functioning body and a contented mind. Horses on the move most of the time, or at least during many hours a day, are naturally going to be stronger, fitter, calmer and better balanced (both mentally and physically), than others denied this right.

Risks can be reduced by turning horses out only with friends on safe ground inside safe fencing, by using feed and water containers with no sharp corners, and by ensuring that no potentially dangerous items or equipment are left in the field. Horses can be booted for protection, and rugged up if it is genuinely cold and wet. So, put the risk into perspective and let your horse have his time out with his friends. The more he gets used to it the more the risks recede. After a hard day, other than in really inclement weather, it is the best way for him to wind down and recover. If the horses *want* to come in they will tell you by hanging around the gate or looking miserable – and this applies in extremes of any weather conditions such as wind, rain, sleet, very hot or cold weather and also times when insects are troublesome – a point many owners overlook.

Clothing

If the horse is staying in, rug him up in cold weather *only* as much as will keep him comfortably warm. He should certainly never be hot or wearing heavy rugs which are wearisome and prevent the air getting to his body.

Most horses these days are over-clipped and over-rugged. It is poor horse management to give a horse a more extensive clip than is genuinely needed to keep him comfortable during work, and this is made worse by adding to his discomfort by piling on the rugs in the stable, or over-rugging when turned out. Provided they are warm enough, horses are clearly happier without rugs or bandages. It can actually amount to cruelty to put so much clothing on a horse – particularly heavy items, or any which do not fit, restrict movement and cause pressure and friction – that the horse actually sweats underneath it. Horses can overheat just as we can but do not have the freedom to remove their rugs, so they just have to stand and suffer. This creates damp and even wet rugs, skin irritations, skin diseases and psychological torment. I am sure many of them would be found to be hyperthermic (overheated) if you took their temperatures.

Check under your horse's rugs with the flat of your hand after they have been on a while and see whether the horse feels just warm (which is what you want), or is very warm, hot or even sweating, which are certainly not what you or he wants.

Most horses find soft stable bandages comforting and it is said that four comfortably bandaged legs make the horse as warm as an extra rug, without the weight. I think that knitted woollen bandages are still the best as they are warm and mould to the legs easily. Put them on over padding, of course, unless the bandages themselves are thick and padded, and apply them only so tightly as to stay on safely. If they are tight, even over padding, they can injure the skin and underlying tissues and restrict the circulation. If they are too loose, of course, they can unravel and trip the horse.

Dealing with distress

If the horse breaks out in a sweat some hours after being put away for the night and you are certain that it is not because you have over-rugged him, he was probably more tired, worried or excited – or all three – than you thought, and needs attention. The old advice was to lead him round until he was dry, but this depends on the weather. You can give him a comforting, gentle massage to get his circulation going instead. If he will eat, you could also give him a small, nourishing and easily digested feed of cooked cereals, if he is used to them, or high-energy fibre and sugar beet pulp, and give some more hay or haylage. (One of the problems associated with horses who 'break out' is that they may also go off their feed.) Change his water, try to get some electrolytes into him and rub him down with hay or old towels if he is damp and change his rugs. Permeable, 'breathable' textiles are the logical choice. Attending quietly to their comforts is reassuring to most horses.

If the horse is clearly tired, maybe lying down a lot or not eating or drinking much, you should check his TPR rates carefully and call your vet with the results, with details of his demeanour and asking for advice. If you are not happy about the way he seems to you next day, or indeed at any time, do the same.

Feeding

As a concerned owner (otherwise you would probably not be reading a book like this), you will probably have a carefully worked-out diet for your horse, and be aware of the fact that energy from a fibre source such as grass, hay, haylage or branded and bagged short-chopped forage feeds is generally the best for horses, with carefully rationed cereals and/or oil in the feeds if extra is required. A reasonably fit horse should not be unduly stressed by short journeys with a careful driver, a good lesson or schooling session, an active hack, a pleasure ride, half a day's hunting or some showing or light competition, and his normal diet will be able to cope with these.

However, when a horse has been working harder, even if he is fit for it, more care should be taken to give him easily digested feeds (initially, in small amounts if he is very tired), until he is rested. As mentioned above, branded cereals may be fine, particularly if they have been processed by being cooked (micronized or extruded) and some people still like to boil linseed and boil or steam oats or barley. In some quarters, the traditional bran mash is being used again, even though the quality of today's bran is far below that of a generation ago. High-energy forages are excellent for performance horses of all types, sugar beet pulp has been used as an energy-giving and easily digested succulent feed for many years now, and additives like honey or molasses can provide energy, too.

Whatever you feed your horse after work, the important thing is to make sure that he is used to it already, so that his digestion does not have the added stress of coping with a change of diet. A bran mash once a week, which used to be given habitually, constitutes a change of feed if the horse does not have a little bran in his normal feeds; so do cereals, which should not be suddenly presented in generous amounts after a hard day's work but at no other time. A change in types of fibre can also be particularly difficult for the horse to cope with, because it can easily upset the population of micro-organisms in the hind gut, and digestive upsets can result.

A good, old, general rule is to always reduce the feed before reducing the work, and always increase the work before increasing the feed: this relates mainly to cereals and is a good guide to avoiding overloading the horse with starch-based energy. It is tempting to give the horse larger feeds than normal to get some energy back into him after he has worked hard, but be careful if he is having a rest the next day. It is a good plan to discuss your horse's diet in relation to his work programme with a vet interested in nutrition, or an equine nutritionist (either one working independently or at the firm whose feeds you use); they can help you to choose appropriate normal ingredients and calculate how to change amounts and proportions according to the horse's workload.

SUMMARY – **FINISHING OFF**

- Freedom and grazing with his friends, if at all possible, is an ideal way for a horse to calm down and recuperate after work.

- Clothing can be used depending on the weather and the horse's needs. It is important that he is comfortable; neither cold, nor overloaded with rugs and too warm.

- Check your horse regularly during the evening following his work (and at night if possible), for signs of breaking out in a sweat through excessive tiredness or over-excitement or nervousness. If this happens, treat him as described above.

- Feeding is important and tired horses need easily digested, familiar feed. Your object is to restore his energy and nutrients without overfeeding him over the next day or so, as he recovers his energy levels. Be very sure he always has clean water freely available.

CHAPTER 14

Summaries of formats for different days

The following formats for warming up, working in, working, cooling down and finally warming down are suggestions for:

1. Days when you have plenty of time to devote to your horse, or he is working hard.

2. Days when you have a fair amount of time, or the horse's work level is moderate.

3. Days when you are short of time, or the horse's workload will be lighter.

Constant objectives

Your objectives, with any routine, are:

1. To warm up by getting the circulation going and loosening up the muscles, other soft tissues and joints.

2. To work in by asking the muscles and joints to work harder in the correct way in order to prepare them for the actual work to come.

3. To perform the horse's intended work.

4. To cool him down and restore his temperature, pulse and respiration rates to warm-up levels or below.

5. To warm down in such a way as to calm the horse and treat his muscles, loosening and lengthening them after work when they may be slightly tense

and contracted and, therefore, to ward off muscle pain and stiffness next day and help to lessen the likelihood of injuries in future.

6. To finish off by settling the horse, relaxing, refuelling and making him physically and mentally comfortable and thus able to rest and recuperate effectively.

First routine – hard work/plenty of time

- Warm up and start loosening up by correct leading in hand at walk – long, swinging strides, encouraging the horse to hold his head and neck low – for ten minutes.

- Give him a massage, relaxing or stimulating depending on whether he is excited or otherwise. If you feel more confident just doing massage-type stroking, do this instead.

- Carry out the suppling/loosening up exercises.

- Lead him around again for several minutes to get the feel of his body after this treatment.

- Work in by doing groundwork such as lungeing or long-reining to start raising his pulse rate (and consequently his temperature and respiration) to get his physique working at a higher, more demanding level with increased blood flow, exchange of oxygen and carbon dioxide, and slightly higher body temperature, in preparation for the actual work planned.

- Perform work in hand from the ground, if desired, to get the horse 'together' and working in a correct (never forced) outline and using his muscles in whatever exercises he can do without the burden of weight on his back.

- Carry out mounted working-in exercises similar to the work to come but at a slightly lower level of performance, to prepare his mind and body for this.

- Carry out dismounted stretching exercises to treat the muscles after working in and to prepare them for the actual work, or work the horse in hand over ground-poles.

summary continues ▶

- Walk and trot around for a few minutes whilst waiting for the start of your intended work.

- Carry out the work planned, whether schooling/lesson, active hack or organized ride, competition or other athletic performance.

- Cool down to lower his TPR rates, initially trotting, jogging and walking out under saddle or in hand, next by using 'wash and walk' if the weather is warm enough, also checking for injuries. Otherwise, lead around, perhaps wearing suitable clothing such as permeable medium to light-weight rugs. Offer short drinks (let him choose between electrolyte drinks and plain water if he has become very warm) every ten minutes until he is no longer thirsty.

- Warm down by lungeing as in the warm-up, using raised ground-poles then lowering them. Massage and carry out stretching exercises and finally walking in hand with a loose, free, swinging stride. The horse should be groomed if he is not too tired, paying particular attention to therapeutic body-brushing. He can be wisped if you have not been able to massage him or do the stretching exercises.

- Finish off by settling him down, making him physically comfortable whether turned out or staying in, maybe putting on rugs and bandages, feeding, watering, closely checking TPR rates and general demeanour (behaviour, appetite and thirst).

Second routine – moderate work/fair amount of time

- Warm up and start loosening up by correct leading in hand at walk – long, swinging strides, encouraging the horse to hold his head and neck low – for ten minutes.

- Give him a massage, relaxing or stimulating depending on whether he is excited or otherwise. If you feel more confident just doing massage-type stroking, do this instead. Try to treat the whole body, but concentrate on back, loins, rump and thighs if pressed for time.

summary continues ▶

- Ideally, carry out the suppling/loosening up exercises or work your horse over ground-poles, in hand or on the lunge to create more effort and lift.

- Work in with a little lateral work in hand to engage the muscles used in this work, both forehand and hindquarters.

- Lead him around again for several minutes to get the feel of his body after this treatment.

- Mount and work in under saddle, performing the type of work to be asked for but at a slightly lower level.

- If you have time, do dismounted stretching exercises. If not, free walk and trot over slightly raised ground-poles.

- Walk and gentle trot around until it is time to work.

- Do the work planned.

- Cool down as described for the first routine, depending on the condition of the horse. If 'wash and walk' is not needed or not possible, try to damp-sponge his face and head to refresh him; also sponge any particularly sweaty areas such as the saddle and girth areas and between the buttocks and hind legs. Rug or not, as appropriate.

- Warm down by lungeing and carrying out stretching exercises; massage or wisp, after which lead in hand for a few minutes, head down and swinging along.

- Finish off as described for the first routine.

Third routine – light work/limited time

- Warm up and start loosening up by correct leading in hand at walk – long, swinging strides, encouraging the horse to hold his head and neck low – for ten minutes.

- Give a short massage or stroking treatment to muscle-mass areas, at least the hindquarters and thighs.

- Before tacking up, try to do suppling exercises.

summary continues ▶

- Mount, and walk and trot in an undemanding way, with completely free head and neck, to get the circulation going. This can be done as the first part of a hack.

- Working in can consist of slightly more demanding work to gradually stress the muscles in preparation, done in correct self-balance and outline. Try to do simple lateral work such as turns on and about the forehand and haunches, shoulder-in and shoulder-out.

- Work: the object of your ride.

- Cool down if necessary, at least walking the horse in a long, swinging stride with his head, neck and tail swinging. Dismount and walk in hand with loosened girth, run-up stirrups and reins over horse's head, allowing him to stretch and swing along, with a rug over him, if necessary.

- Warm down and do stretching exercises, if time. Grooming and wisping would be advantageous.

- Finish off as appropriate for the level of work the horse has just completed. Maybe all that will be needed is to turn him out with friends or make him comfortable, as normal, in his box if he is staying in.

Further reading

There are so many excellent horse books available these days that the following can represent only a small selection of those I feel will be of the most interest and help to readers of this book. Some of my own, which are relevant, are included also.

Bromiley, Mary, *Massage For Horses*, Kenilworth Press (Shrewsbury) 1996, ISBN 1-872082-87-4

Hannay, Pamela, *Shiatsu Therapy for Horses*, J.A. Allen (London) 2002, ISBN 0-85131-847-9

Henderson, Carolyn, *Getting Horses Fit*, J.A. Allen (London) 2006, ISBN-10: 0-85131-897-5, ISBN-13: 978-0-85131-897-4

Gray, Peter, *Essential Care of the Ridden Horse*, David & Charles (Newton Abbot) 2002, ISBN 0-7153-1158-1

McBane, Susan, *Fitness in the Horse*, Crowood Press (Marlborough) 1996, ISBN 1-85223-963-8

McBane, Susan, *How Your Horse Works*, David & Charles (Newton Abbot) 1996, ISBN 0-7153-0861-0

McBane, Susan, *Bodywork For Horses: techniques you can use yourself*, Sportsman's Press (Shrewsbury) 2005, ISBN 1-904057-48-9

McBane, Susan, *100 Ways To Improve Your Horse's Health*, David & Charles (Newton Abbot) 2005, ISBN 0-7153-2001-7

Sutton, Amanda, *The Injury-Free Horse*, David & Charles (Newton Abbot) 2001,
ISBN 0-7153-1100-X

Stanier, Sylvia, *The Art of Lungeing*, J. A. Allen (London) 1993,
ISBN 0-85131-573-9

Stanier, Sylvia, *The Art of Long Reining*, J. A. Allen (London) 1995,
ISBN 0-85131-574-7

Useful contacts

Association of Chartered Physiotherapists in Animal Therapy
Tel: 01962 863801, website: www.acpat.org.uk

Sarah Fisher, TTEAM UK (Tellington Touch Equine Awareness Method)
Tel: 01761 471128, website: www.ttouchtteam.co.uk

The Classical Riding Club
Fax: 01890 830667, website: www.classicalriding.co.uk

The Equine Behaviour Forum
Tel: 01254 705487, website: www.gla.ac.uk/External/EBF/

The Equine Shiatsu Association
Tel: 01903 814860, website: www.equineshiatsuassociation.com

The Equine Sports Massage Association
Tel: 01285 650275, website: www.equinemassageassociation.co.uk

Index